A Teen's Guide to Finding a Job!

D1382809

Naomi Vernon
Youth Career Counselor

Second Edition

New-Bee-ginnings, San Antonio, Texas

ISBN: 1-4033-1140-4 (e-book)
ISBN: 1-4033-1141-2 (Paperback)

This book is printed on acid free paper.

1stBooks – rev. 11/25/02

More Endorsements...

☆ *A Teen's Guide to Finding a Job* is all encompassing and offers the high school teacher the structure to take students through the job process from assessment to interviews! For high schools who do not offer a job developer's assistance, this book will be extremely helpful.
Ms. Claudia O'Leary, Principal
Academy for Career Education

☆ As a teenager who has been out looking for a job, I know that having read this book gave me an "edge" by helping me to understand what an employer is looking for.
Paul Henri
Inspired Air Force Academy Student

☆ *A Teen's Guide to Finding a Job* is an excellent source for teenagers who have no one to guide them through the "job search process." You'll learn how to find out more about your "workself" and it provides great untraditional tips on how to find employment you will be happy with. It simplifies the process.
Mr. Charlie Greanoff
Ombudsmen Coordinator

☆ *A Teen's Guide to Finding a Job* offers solid, concise advice on how to secure a good job and launch a career. While directed at a teen audience, the book provides valuable counsel to people of all ages who desire productive and satisfying employment.
G. James Olsen, Author
President, Preuma

Endorsements continued...

☆ *A Teen's Guide to Finding a Job* is a "must read" book for all teens seeking employment. A very comprehensive, step-by-step guide to obtaining employment. It is very well thought out and organized. The book can be an excellent resource for teachers to use in business classes.
Robert A. Diehl
Relocation Assistance Program Manager
Department of Defense

☆ Finding a job in this fast-paced world of change can even be puzzling to adults. Reading *A Teen's Guide to Finding a Job* and then giving it to your teenager can help both of you make career decisions and develop job search strategies that create success and happiness in your work and life.
Cook Consultants
Kaye Cook Designer and Facilitator
A career workshop for teens... MY COMPANY, INC.

☆ The book really helped me, especially on how to act during an interview for a job. I found tips on how to look and speak impressively. And the book explained a lot about the employer's needs that I didn't understand or realize before.
Rona May Datu
Student

☆ The book was very informative and will help anyone looking for a career, not just a job. The book also shared things that are demanded in the workforce and are essential to know.
Mi Song (Shawna) Smith
Student

Who You'll See Inside ...

Carlos

Nikki

Sophia

Bill

David

Candiss

What You'll Learn Inside ...

☆ Self-assessment

☆ Employment application

☆ Interviewing techniques

☆ Salary Negotiation

☆ Research

☆ Résumé writing

☆ Employer's perspective

☆ Resignation

Introduction

You may not be clear about your career goals or objectives. Or you may know what you want to be when you grow up, but don't know how to make it happen. Many times you are exposed to the myths and horror tales of other's experiences with the job search process, so that even before you begin looking for a job or deciding on a career you are confused. Your view of the job search process may have been tainted by fear of rejection, lack of self-knowledge, and being unfamiliar with the many job search techniques. This teen guide will help you clarify the steps you need to take when making a career decision, or applying for a limited or full-time job.

Carlos

Beginning a career search or looking for a job can be a most rewarding experience if you have the proper tools and information at your fingertips. This handbook will provide you the tools to build skills and put you on the road to future employment.

Remember, your first job could be the foundation for your chosen career as you enter into this exciting time of your life.

Acknowledgements

*First and foremost I give thanks to my heavenly
and divine Father for blessing the writing of this book.*

This book could not have been written without the support of my loving husband and best friend Kenneth E. Vernon, Sr., my two beautiful sons, Kenneth E. Vernon, Jr. and David Mozell Vernon.

Warm thanks to my niece/daughter Sophia ReNa Morris.

Also Shirley Morris, my sister by blood and sorority, "Zeta Phi Beta."

A host of thanks to a host of dear friends: Cathy Knight, Renee Lane, Giles Hudson, Marva Campbell, Telisa Cureton, Shawna Johnson, Pat Stokes, Dave Lynch, Bill and Maureen Sherman, Marilyn Mitchell and many more.

A special thanks to Judith E. Ball for layout and design, and Billy R. Ball and Susana Luzier for providing unconditional assistance.

Thank you Candiss Caldwell for offering your creative talents and Mark Buchanan for your artistic front cover layout.

Thanks to Kaye Cook of Cook's Consultants for your guidance and advice.

I especially thank Nancy Taylor and Irene Spears, close family members and my big sisters in "Zeta Phi Beta."

This book is dedicated to

my loving parents Roger D. and Essie L. Morris, and my Aunt and Uncle Nelson and Johnselene Blunt, for teaching me that life has no limits and that I can do and be whatever I desire. To my brothers Roger D. Morris, Jr., A. C. Morris, Fred Morris, Robert Morris, Ernest Donaldson, Roosevelt Donaldson, and my sister Beverland Melton for shaping my thoughts and beliefs. To Fred Morris, Jr. and Sharaun Settles, (my nephews by blood, but my true brothers in love, I am so proud of the two of you). Last, but not forgotten: to Howard Vernon, my loving father-in-law, who loves me unconditionally, and to the three best in-laws in the world; Julie Wade Selmon, Barbara Johnson, and the late Howard Vernon , Jr.

About the Author

Life's situations and sympathetic feelings inspired the author, Naomi Vernon, to write this book. As a young person not knowing much about the world of work and observing how others reacted to their job search experiences her understanding and compassion were heightened for these people. She was also fascinated by the power this process could have over an individual's life, and this is what prompted her to pursue a life's commitment in the Human Resources career field.

Through personal encounters and carefully studying the "job search process" she recognized that stress and negativity could be experienced by a person of any age while looking for employment. She concluded it was caused partially by the lack of self-knowledge, a fear of rejection, as well as being unfamiliar with job search techniques.

Mrs. Vernon has spent hundreds of hours volunteering with America's youth. Introducing and preparing them for the same job search process as detailed in each of these chapters. She also provides guidance and counseling to her own sons. Her goals for this guide are to equip the youth of America with the tools needed to succeed, to increase their awareness, and inspire them to go after their dreams. Hopefully, after reading this guide and completing the assignments anyone will view the job search process as adventurous, exciting and a positive experience. And most of all they will welcome the challenge!

Mrs. Vernon has a Master of Arts Degree in Human Resources Development, and certification from California registry of Professional Counselors, and Paraprofessional Counselors, a division of California's Association for "Career" Counseling and Development (CACD).

Contents

Who You'll See Inside i

What You'll Learn Inside i

Introduction iii

Acknowledgements v

Dedications vi

About the Author vii

Table of Contents ix

Chapter 1:   Self-assessment Tools 1

Overview 3
    What self-assessments can do 4
    What self-assessments cannot do 5
    Understanding the results of a self-assessment .. 5
The various types of self-assessments 6
Where you can get self-assessment and career
planning information 8
    Other resources that may offer
    self-assessments 8

On-line resources of self-assessments 9
Your personal action plan 11

Chapter 2: Research 15

Overview 17
Informational interviewing 18
    You may choose to conduct informational
      interviews 19
    What you should know before conducting
      informational interviews 19
    Things you should do 20
    Script for conducting informational
    interviews 21
    Informational interviewing tips 22
    Possible questions you might ask 23
Reading 26
Networking 28
    To prepare yourself for networking 29
    Your 30-second networking commercial 29
    Networking tips 30
    Networking chart 32
Career fairs 33
    Career fair preparation 33
    Career fair do's 34
    Career fair don'ts 35
Your 60-second introduction 36

Chapter 3: The Employment Application Process 39

Overview 41
Appearance 43
Content.. 44
Validity 44
Completing an employment application.................. 45
A sample application form 49
Verbs and power words 51
  Helping skills 51
  Communication skills 52
  Detail skills... 52
  Teaching skills 53
  Research skills 53
  Management skills 54
  Technical skills 55
  Financial skills 55
  Manual skills.. 56
  Creative skills 56
  Problem solving skills... 57
  Discriminative skills 58
  Laboratory skills 59
  Computer language skills 60
Application tips.. 62
You can do it 62

Chapter 4: Résumés 65

Overview 67
Let's begin
  Your résumé is a reflection of you 70

Getting started 70
   Your headings 71
   Your career objective 71
   Your work experience 72
   Your training 72
   Your education... 72
   Your work history 73
   Optional heading 74
Choosing a format... 76
   The chronological résumé 76
      The advantages 76
      The disadvantages................................ 77
      Sample of a chronological résumé 78
   The functional résumé 79
      The advantages 79
      The disadvantages................................ 80
      Sample of a functional résumé 81
   The combination résumé 82
      The advantages 82
      The disadvantages................................ 83
      Sample of a combination résumé 84
Résumé guidelines 85
   The résumé format.................................... 85
   Résumé content... 86
   General tips... 86
Writing a cover letter 88
   Three basic techniques for writing a
      cover letter.. 88
   Letter content 89
   Sample of a cover letter............................. 92
Preparing a reference sheet 93

Chapter 5: Interviewing 97

Overview 99
The interviewing process 100
    Interviewing strategies 103
    Research networking 103
    People 104
    Written materials 104
    "Acing" the interview 105
        Education 106
        Work Experience 107
        Career Goals 107
        Personality and Other Concerns 108
    Tips for preparing thank you letters 110
    The body of your thank you letter 110
    Sample of a thank you letter 111

Chapter 6: The Employer's Perspective 113

Overview 115
    The application and résumé *do* list 117
    The interview *do* list 118
    The application *do not* list 119
    The interview *do not* list 120
    The *do not* list after you are hired 122
    Words of wisdom and encouraging messages ... 123
Job search skills 125
    Communication skills 125
    Transferable skills 125
    Body language 126

Chapter 7: Salary Negotiation 131

Overview 133
Good ethical practices 134
Know your work values 135
Current work values that are
important to you.......................................135

Chapter 8: If You Must Quit a Job..................139

Overview 141
How to get out of a bad situation..........141
Sample of a resignation letter 144

Conclusion..................147

Overview 149

Quick Reference to

Research and Reading Material..................151

The various types of self-assessment
tools...152
On-line resources of self-assessments 153
Reading..154

Order Form 155

Practice Application Form 156

Chapter 1
Self-assessment Tools

Nikki

Chapter 1
Self-assessment Tools

Overview

The first thing you should do is take a self-assessment. It is a way you can inventory your skills, interests, knowledge and abilities, work values and personal traits. It will increase your awareness of the skills you are already using daily at home, in school, and in the community. It can match you to a job or career most suitable for your personality. Knowing who you are and how you fit into the world of work will help you select a rewarding job and career. A self-assessment will prevent you from making choices based on someone else's values or expectations.

There are a variety of self-assessment tools you can use. Some self-assessment tools may consist of you answering a series of questions. There are no right or wrong answers. Your scores are based on a pattern of answers, not your answer to any particular question. Your choice of answers should reflect what you actually do, and what you really feel, so be honest; there is no way you can fail. Most importantly, self-assessment results will provide you

options to explore. They will give you information about
yourself that you probably do not know or place any
value on. When applied properly the information from
your assessment can play a major role in helping to find
the job or career path that is perfect for you.

What self-assessments can do

A self-assessment can help you find the job or career
path that fits you and will prevent you from finding one
that you will not be comfortable with. It is a good tool
used to encourage self-exploration. Finding a job or
career that is right for your personality will make you
happy, fulfilled, and satisfied with your career choices.
Lack of preparation and self-knowledge is the main reason most people are unhappy with their jobs. They find
themselves in jobs or careers not fitting to their personality. It can cause one to be unhappy, depressed, and
even unhealthy. A self-assessment will help assess your
likes and dislikes. It measures the similarity of your likes
and dislikes to people who are successfully working in
various occupations that will be available to you.

When you have similar interests to people successfully
employed in a career field research has proven that you
will be satisfied working in that field also.

What self-assessments cannot do

A self-assessment cannot tell you what you are going to be. It can only provide you with information about careers that will be best suited to you. You know yourself better than anyone else. You must compare the results to what you know about yourself.

For example you are very good in math and your self-assessment results suggested you become a mathematician, but you know you like working more with people. That is a clue for you to explore your career options, to look for those jobs or careers that will allow you to work more with people while still using your math skills. The results of the self-assessment give you choices. You can explore those choices. Only after completing your research should you begin making career decisions.

Understanding the results of a self-assessment

You should view the results of a self-assessment as options *only*. The results are not what you should become, unless it is what you really want to be. Remember, self-assessments give information about yourself that you probably already knew but took for granted or did not value.

The various types of self-assessment tools

Any of the assessments listed below are great tools to help you become more aware of your skills, interests, work values, and personal traits.

CAREER ABILITY PLACEMENT SURVEY (CAPS) —
Is a series of tests measuring eight specific areas of *ability*. The eight areas are: Mechanical Reasoning, Spatial Relations, Verbal Reasoning, Numerical Ability, Language Usage, Word Knowledge, Perceptual Speed and Accuracy, and Manual Speed and Dexterity.

CAREER OCCUPATIONAL PREFERENCE SURVEY
(COPS) SYSTEM —
The COPS System measures abilities, interests, and values. The scores are related to fourteen occupational groupings or clusters. It consists of a series of activities related to occupations. You should honestly answer the questions based on your likes and dislikes. It is best used for college-bound and vocationally oriented people.

CAREER ORIENTATION PLACEMENT AND EVALUATION SURVEY
(COPES) —
Designed to measure personal values. Constructing a set of work values and qualities will help you choose a career that will give you a sense of purpose and meaning. Work values are part of a larger framework of life values.

EDUCATIONAL INTEREST INVENTORY —
Is designed to assist junior and senior high school students, freshman and sophomore college students, vocational and technical students, and adult continuing

education students by assessing their interests and relating it to collegiate and vocational study.

KEIRSEY TEMPERAMENT SORTER —
Is designed to identify different kinds of personality temperaments.

MYERS-BRIGGS TYPE INDICATOR (MBTI) —
Used for assisting individuals with identifying their preferences, how they view things and make decisions. Knowing your own preferences and learning about others can help you understand your strengths, the type of work you might enjoy and be successful doing, and how others with different preferences can *relate to each other and be of value to one another.*

SELF-DIRECTED SEARCH —
A self-guided assessment that helps you find the occupations and fields of study best suited to your interests and skills. You answer questions about preferred activities, competencies, occupations, and abilities. Based on your answers you will receive a three-letter summary code. The code tells you what occupations your personality is best suited for and the types of work or training programs that match your interests.

THE STRONG INTEREST INVENTORY —
Gives you information about your interests in relation to the interests of people working in the actual occupation. The focus is to help you better understand yourself so that you can make better decisions about selecting academic majors and careers.

Where you can get self-assessment and career planning information

The first stop should be your school Guidance Counselor. He or she will explain which assessments are available for you to use, as well as explain the objective of each, and suggest what assessment would be best for identifying your needs and most appropriate for your situation. Your counselor may have other books and computer programs you can use to further explore your career interests. The counselor can help you plan for your future career by helping you select the classes you need to take to prepare for your chosen career field or to further your education.

Other resources that may offer the services of administering self-assessments

Agencies:

☆ Employment Agencies

☆ High School Guidance Counselors

☆ Career Counselors

☆ Social Services Agencies

☆ Placement and Job Referral Services

☆ National Career Development Association (NCDA)

☆ Career Information Centers

☆ State Employment Services

On-line resources of self-assessments

Careers By Design
On-line Assessment Center. Identifying your general interest. http://www.careers-by-design.com/p13.htm

Cook Consultants Designer and Facilitator
A career workshop for teens... MY COMPANY, INC.
Kcooknet@aol.com

JobHuntersBible.com
Excellent tool for researching companies, obtaining salary information, and has excellent site links.
http://www.jobhuntersbible.com/research/research.shtml

High School Student
Best used for students looking for a job after graduation or planning to continue with their education. The SIGI Plus will help you put your career plans in order.
http://www.ets.org/sigi/hsstudnt.html

The Temperament Sorter II
Discovering Your Personality
http://www.advisorteam.com/user/ktsintro.asp

Myers-Briggs Type Indicator
Helps you understand your preferences and those of others.
http://www.mbti.com/products/mbti/index.asp

Note: The Myers-Briggs Type Indicator can not be taken on the Internet. The instrument can only be administered by licensed institutions and organizations.

Self-Directed Search
Most widely used career interest inventory. Discover Holland (RIASEC) code and match your skills and interests to a job, career, training program, college major, and fields of study. http://www.self-directed-search.com/sdsreprt.html

Strong Interest Inventory
Books. http://www.christiancareercenter.com/guidance/strong.shtml

Tech Prep
For students to prepare for a "high-skill" career while still in high school. It is designed to give students academic and work-related skills.
http://www.ets.org/sigi/s2.html

There are many other self-assessment tools on the market, so take your time in selecting the one that is right for you. Your goal is to select the one which will meet your needs. Visit your school Guidance Counselor. (Again don't be afraid to visit your school's Guidance Counselor.)

Your personal action plan

Completed my research and decided to take the self-assessment _____.

(Type of assessment)

I will contact _____
to schedule my appointment for taking the assessment.

Date and time my self-assessment is scheduled
_____.

My self-assessment results found _____
_____
_____.

I am interested in the following: _____
_____
_____.

I will research _____
_____
_____.

This is the direction I plan to take _____

_____

_____

_____.

My career choices are_____

_____

_____

_____.

*Self-assessments are important
because you must know who you are
before you can decide what to become...*

Chapter 2
Research

Dictionary of
Occupational Titles

American Almanac
of Jobs & Salaries

Occupational
Outlook Handbook

Directory of
Directories

Di

Di

Encyclopedia of
Business Information

Occupational
Outlook Quarterly

Guide for Occupational
Exploration

David

Chapter 2
Research

Overview

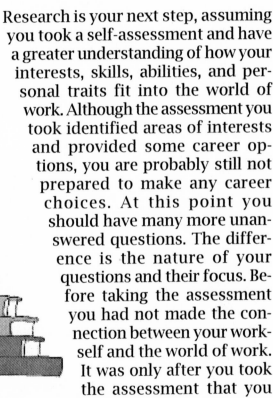

Research is your next step, assuming you took a self-assessment and have a greater understanding of how your interests, skills, abilities, and personal traits fit into the world of work. Although the assessment you took identified areas of interests and provided some career options, you are probably still not prepared to make any career choices. At this point you should have many more unanswered questions. The difference is the nature of your questions and their focus. Before taking the assessment you had not made the connection between your work-self and the world of work. It was only after you took the assessment that you made the connection. Most likely, you now know the type of work you are interested in or probably what you want to become. Yet, no career choices should be made until other facts are considered. It is best to have a complete profile before making any career choices.

Your goal is to learn as much as you can about the career field or job of your interest. You must gather information that will help you see the complete picture. There are some important things you need to know before making a career choice, such as higher education requirements, related occupations, training and certification requirements, and the academic curriculum pre-paratory requirements.

In addition, it is important to know the job demographics (which are the *components* of a job), such as the work conditions, environment, working hours, wages or salary paid, and whether or not the job will support the lifestyle you hope to have. Getting a complete profile before applying for a job will keep you from frequently changing jobs and being unhappy. You must research to get the information that is needed to make smart career choices. Research can be done in a variety of ways. In this guide we will discuss the most effective ways for getting your questions answered.

Informational interviewing

Interviewing is a great way to get answers to your questions and meet interesting people. It provides the opportunity for you to make direct contact with people already working in the job or career field of your choice. When conducting information interviews you are going directly to the source to get answers to your career questions.

You may choose to conduct informational interviews

☆ To get information that will help you make smart career choices.

☆ To get accurate and current information about the industry, career field, salary, and job of your choice.

☆ To get an understanding of a company, organization, and job structure.

☆ To increase your knowledge of job duties and responsibilities.

☆ To become knowledgeable about information that is useful for preparing your application and résumé.

☆ To get advice on the direction of your academic curriculum, volunteer opportunities, and career choices.

What you should know before conducting informational interviews

Conducting informational interviews may require you to work outside of your comfort zone. At first you may feel a little uncomfortable, but the more practice you get the easier it is to do, and the more relaxed you'll become. Basically, we live in a friendly world with people who enjoy talking about themselves and what they do. For the most part, people will be helpful and very happy to assist you. If you encounter rejection don't take it personally; sometimes people with complex work schedules will not take the extra time to stop and help you. Just keep focused and continue calling. Remember informational interviewing will build your confidence in knowing the match between yourself and the job. It will expand your knowledge of the job, provide the opportunity for you to meet interesting new people, and give you access to current information. It can make a significant impact on the effectiveness of your job search. It can make the difference between finding an acceptable job and getting the job of your dreams. You may want to start with family members, neighbors, friends, and your parents for practice. It is worth stretching yourself. So get started!

Things you should do

1. **Call people direct** if possible. Before calling, make sure you have their name and exact job title.

2. **Ask permission for their time** before you proceed to engage them in conversation. If necessary make an appointment with them.

3. **Explain the reason for your call.** If someone else recommended that you call, give that person's name.

4. **Have paper and pencil handy** so you can write down the important things, those things you want to remember as a result of the conversation.

5. **Make sure you get their mailing address** so you can follow up with a thank you note.

Script for conducting informational interviews

1. **Identify yourself.** "Hello. I am a student at (*state your school name*). I am doing some research on (*state the job title or career of your interest*).

2. **Get the person's name.** "Can you tell me the person's name who does (*state job title or career interest*)? Write the person's name down.

3. **Ask to speak with that person.** "May I speak with (*state their name*)?"

   If the receptionist will not put your call through, thank her/him and hang up. Write down the time and go to the next call. Call back later (wait at least one hour). When you call back make sure you ask for the person by name. However, if your call gets through the first time reintroduce yourself. Don't expect people to re-member you until they get to know you.

4. **Greet the person.** "Good (*morning/afternoon*) Mr./Mrs._____. May I have 15 minutes of your time to ask a few questions about your career/job? I'm interested in (*state the job title or career field*) and would like to know (*state what you want to know*)."

   — or —

   "Mr./Mrs. _____ would you prefer we meet in person?"
   If their preference is to meet with you, schedule a day and time that is convenient for them. You must be flexible. Otherwise, if given permission to proceed,

or you sense it is all right to continue, begin asking your questions.

5. **Close by expressing your appreciation.** Ask for the correct spelling of their name and get their address so you can send a thank you note right away.

6. **Prepare and send a thank you note.** Immediately following the informational interview take the time to write a sincere note of appreciation.

Informational interviewing tips

1. Prepare a script and a list of questions before calling. This way you will present yourself as being organized, serious, and prepared. People are more willing to help you.

2. Correctly pronounce the person's name you are trying to reach, using their *formal name* (Mr. or Mrs. Ball) in most situations. Practice pronouncing it before calling, this will show that you care enough to be informed of the person's title and status.

3. Speak clearly and confidently. It implies that you know exactly what you want.

4. Stick to the time frame you've agreed upon, to show respect for their time.

5. Have pen and paper handy. This will help you keep calm, while also showing that you are prepared to listen and even take notes if necessary.

6. Ask for the names of other people who might provide additional information. You will be surprised at the helpful responses you receive.

7. Don't give up too quickly. The more you practice, the easier the art of interviewing and being interviewed becomes.

Possible questions you might ask

1. What skill, knowledge, or experience are required to qualify for your position?

2. What type of formal, specialized, or higher education do you have?

3. What educational advice would you have for someone interested in your job or career field?

4. What other experience or training would be helpful for the job?

5. Could you describe your typical day at work?

6. What do you like most about your current job?

7. In your position when making decisions how much freedom do you have?

8. Are there related fields I should explore?

9. What is the starting salary?

10. What are the possible career paths in your field of work?

11. Would you make the same career choice again? Why or why not?

12. Describe your physical work environment?

13. What do you dislike about your current job?

14. Do you work as a team member or independently?

15. What does the future hold for your job?

16. Where is most of your work done? (Inside or outside?)

17. Do you offer a *shadowing* program? If so, may I shadow *you* for a day?

    Explanation: A *"student shadowing program"* is provided by many businesses to give you, the student, direct exposure to the job you seem interested in. For a specified amount of time you will be *partnered* with an employee experienced in that position, and you will be permitted to see the basic daily duties, the job environment, and its common practices. Once the program is completed, you will know better if this is the type of work you want to pursue.

18. Would you describe your working conditions?

19. How did you acquire your current position?

20. What keeps you interested in your work?

21. What does it take to become successful in your job?

22. How is your job different than what it appears to an outsider?

23. Do you know anyone else I should or could talk with?

Reading

Reading is a valuable way to obtain information about a job or career field. The public library or your school career center should have books, publications, directories, and articles that contain information on jobs, careers, and industry trends. Read a variety of materials to get many different views and opinions.

AMERICAN ALMANAC OF JOBS & SALARIES
Published by Avon Books, New York. Gives wages for specific occupations and job groups — many are professional and white collar. It also covers employment and wage trends.

DICTIONARY OF OCCUPATIONAL TITLES, "DOT"
Published by the Department of Labor. It groups over 20,000 jobs into major categories. Describes the general requirements of each grouping.

DIRECTORY OF DIRECTORIES
Lists directories alphabetically. Also classifies directories according to subject.

ENCYCLOPEDIA OF ASSOCIATIONS
Lists over 22,000 professional, trade, and other nonprofit organizations in the U.S.

GUIDE FOR OCCUPATIONAL EXPLORATION
Published by the Department of Labor. Groups the 20,000 jobs in the DOT under 12 general interest areas.

OCCUPATIONAL OUTLOOK HANDBOOK, "OOH"
Published by the U.S. Department of Labor and Bureau

of Labor Statistics. Tells about 300 or more kinds of jobs in terms of requirements, skills needed, kinds of employers who hire, work conditions, and advancement potential. Lists the 225 most popular jobs where 80 percent of all people work. It's updated every two years.

OCCUPATIONAL OUTLOOK QUARTERLY
Published by the U.S. Department of Labor. Gives overview of the outlook for different sectors of the economy and individual occupations. May contain featured articles on the particular selected job area.

O'NET DICTIONARY OF OCCUPATIONAL TITLES
Designed to update and replace the Dictionary of Occupational Titles (DOT). Describes approximately 1200 jobs covering nearly 100 percent of the United States workforce. It includes information on earnings, education, tasks, skills related jobs and much more.

Excellent Internet Sites

SNAGAJOB.COM at (www.snagajob.com)
Locate part-time, temporary, and summer employment. The Job Seeker Resource Center offers assistance with preparing resumes and perfecting interviewing techniques. Find job hunting tips, post résumés, and get your career questions answered.

SUMMERJOBS.COM at (www.summerjobs.com)
Review nationwide summer job opportunities. Take a free on-line career assessment, review job hunting tips, and sign up to receive a career newsletter.

Networking

Networking is the intentional exchange of knowledge, skills, information, resources, and/or contacts that is of immediate or future benefit to all parties involved.
(This networking definition was supplied by Kaye Cook.)

Networking begins with people you have direct contact with and knowledge of.

An example of networking: Ask a trusted teacher, or someone else you respect, to recommend individuals you may contact to get your career questions answered. If your request is granted and you are supplied with leads, get permission to use the referring person's name.

Through networking you can gain knowledge not publicly known, get valuable leads, and broaden your contacts. Networking is a way to get specific information that will help you make smart career choices. It can be an excellent research tool.

Do not begin networking until you have clearly defined your objectives.

To prepare yourself for networking

You should know...   your interests, skills, and abilities.

You should know...   the career fields your *work-self* closely matches.

You should know...   what questions you want to ask your contacts.

You should know...   the best place to start networking, then proceed to do so.

Your 30-second networking commercial

"Hello, my name is_____

I am good at_____ and _____.
                    Your greatest interests.

I am interested in the career field of _____.
                                    Your career choice.

I could be good in this career because I like to do _____, _____, and _____.

Do you know of anyone interested in_____that
                                Same type of career choice.

may help me with this career choice?"

Networking tips

☆ Know what information you want to gain from people you are networking with. It shows respect of their time, as well as showing that you are well organized and prepared.

☆ Identify individuals you feel comfortable talking to and sharing with. It will immediately make you feel more comfortable to express your thoughts.

☆ Organize your thoughts and questions, so you present yourself as someone who knows exactly what he/she wants and gives the impression that you are committed.

☆ Ask your contacts for additional leads, such as recommendations for actions and suggestions for future contacts. You might be surprised how much this will increase your networking system.

☆ Get permission to use the referring person's name, if you feel the person is valued and respected. It may encourage the person you are attempting to reach to open up and share information with you.

☆ Maintain records of your contacts, listing specific information about each. This way you will be able to keep track of the most important facts of your research for future use.

☆ Keep all appointments, agreements, and promises.

☆ Keep an open line of communication built upon trust with your networking contacts. Be honest; people will appreciate it by being more willing to help you.

☆ Always send thank you notes. This simple act will show your appreciation, besides it will help to keep you on their mind for a future opening.

☆ Continue to repeat the process until you have obtained your goals. Don't be discouraged, nor afraid of hearing the word, "No." Continue to reach for your goals, because eventually your persistence will pay off.

☆ Remember that networking is both giving and taking. When people help you, you look for opportunities to help others in return.

Research Carefully

Networking chart

Using this chart will help you identify in advance the individuals you think may have valuable information. It should quicken your ability to pinpoint the best places and people to begin networking with.

Also, putting your plans on paper will make it easier for you to act upon your goals, keep track of your contacts, and the role they play in your plans.

1. Family Members:

_____

_____

_____

_____

_____

2. Teachers:

_____

_____

_____

_____

_____

3. Community Leaders:

_____

_____

_____

_____

4. Local Merchants:

_____

_____

_____

_____

Career fairs

Career fairs may be used as a tool for gathering information. Attending a career fair for the first time can be overwhelming. There will be representatives from many businesses ready and willing to talk with you. They will be fully prepared to answer your questions and ask several of their own. That's why it is important for you to prepare yourself for meeting and talking with a large variety of employers.

You can go to your school counselor, your local chamber of commerce, local colleges and universities, and even technical schools for information on local fairs in your area or the company sponsoring the fair.

Career fair preparation

Your goal is to gather information that will help you make smart career choices. Attending a career fair is an excellent way to get your questions answered. Employers are there to share information about their company, to answer your questions, and provide any assistance that will increase your knowledge about the company and recruit potential employees.

1. The first thing to do, if possible, is get a list of employers attending the fair. Often they are listed in the local newspaper.

2. Next, familiarize yourself with the employer's mission, product, and services. You can obtain this infor-

mation from the Internet. Organize your thoughts and make a list of questions you want to ask each employer. Carry a notebook for storing handouts, pamphlets, flyers, and other materials received from employers.

3. Finally, prepare a 60-second introduction. (See example on page 36.)

Career fair dos

1. **Dress professionally.** First impressions are lasting. You should dress as if you were being interviewed for a job. Your clothes must be clean, carefully pressed, and neat. No excess jewelry, no baggy pants, nor baseball caps.

2. **Be friendly.** Greet each employer with a smile and a firm handshake.

3. **Be prepared.** Have a list of questions to ask and a résumé to give to employers.

4. **Be independent.** Leave your friends at home. You want to appear mature, capable, and willing. Your appearance should radiate great potential.

5. **Relax.** Be friendly and have a sense of humor. Be prepared to hold intelligent and interesting conversations.

6. **Closure.** Close by giving thanks for their time and leaving with a smile.

Career fair don'ts

1. **Don't be afraid to talk with employers.** They are there to talk with you and to be helpful. This is the perfect time to get all of your questions answered.

2. **Don't use slang or negative words.** It will leave a very negative impression about your attitude.

3. **Don't waste the employer's time.** Be articulate and get straight to the point. Have your thoughts mentally organized.

4. **Don't be impolite.** Wait your turn to speak. Do not invite yourself into another's conversation. Listen and learn.

5. **Don't share your personal experiences with employers.** This is not the time to form lasting friendships. (Your personal situation should remain just that — *personal*. Sharing personal information can lead to wrong impressions.) Remember you are there to get your *career* questions answered. *Remain focused.*

Your 60-second introduction

"Hi, my name is _____.
$\qquad\qquad\qquad\qquad\qquad$ (state your name)

I am a student at _____.
$\qquad\qquad\qquad\qquad\qquad$ (identify your school)

I am interested in_____.
$\qquad\qquad\qquad\qquad$ (state the job title you are interested in)

Today, I am gathering information that will help me make some career choices. I am interested in this type of work because _____,

_____, and _____.
(Share at least three reasons why you are interested in this particular career field.)

May I have a few minutes of your time to ask questions?"

List of questions you may want to ask:

1. Does your company have a need for my type of work?

2. Please explain what your company's career path is for my particular interest in _____.

3. What type of skills do you recruit for my particular interest?

4. What is the starting salary _____?

Research is exploring today's options,
which may lead into tomorrow's possibilities...

Chapter 3
The Employment
Application Process

Sophia

Chapter 3

The Employment Application Process

Overview

The employment application process is very critical to your job search. It begins when you enter the employer's place of business to request an employment application and ends with the interview. The employment application is the link between you and the employer. It is the employer's first formal introduction to you. Remember, these first impressions are based on the information listed on your employment application, as well as the manner in which you present it.

A good employment application will get you to the next step, the interview. Employers use the employment application to screen you out of the interviewing process. How you complete the employment application will tell the employer many things about you. For instance, leaving areas blank gives the impression you did not read the entire application. It may lead the employer to believe that you will rush through your work, and that you may not complete assignments or tasks. Avoid scratching out information when making a mistake. It gives a sloppy appearance. It may imply you are not a conscientious worker and that your work or appearance is not important to you.

Just by the content and appearance of your employment application the employer will determine whether or not to give you an interview. The employment application typically covers four important points for the employer:

1.   Who you are.
2.   What your present or past work experience is.
3.   What you can do.
4.   When you are available to do it.

The employment application is a tool you may use to make a good first impression. Most importantly, you want the employer to know you have the skills to do the job, your related experiences to that job, and your accomplishments. The employment application is the avenue you will use to get that information to the employer. You may demonstrate it through words of expression. Your chances of making a good first impression on the application will improve by being aware of its appearance, content, and validity.

By the way, you will find that many companies *require* you to complete their employment application, because it is a legal document which can be upheld in court. Once you sign and date an employment application you are saying that everything on it is true. You can be fired from a job if they find out that you lied on the application.

Appearance

The application and your physical appearance tell the employer many things. When you walk into the employer's place of business to pick up the employment application people will begin to form opinions about you. They want to know who you are, how you heard about the job opening, whether you are qualified, and most importantly how you will fit in. You are being sized up at this time.

Impressions are being formed based on how you are dressed, the way you talk, and even how you walk. Therefore, when picking up the employment application you should dress appropriately. Give special attention to your personal hygiene. Use deodorant, and all perfumes and colognes should be used conservatively. Camouflage any tattoos. Your hair should be washed and styled. Your clothes should be clean, neatly pressed, and suitable. Casual clothing, such as, baggy pants, t-shirts, mini-dresses, shorts, or sleeveless clothing should not be worn when looking for employment. It all reflects an unprofessional image.

Respect is what you want to earn with your clothing: you want to be chosen based on your skills, not turned away because you wore trendy or inappropriate clothing. It is important to use proper English, with absolutely no slang. The way you walk should radiate confidence; hold your head up high and be proud, give a firm handshake and make direct eye contact. The completed employment application form should be neat: there should be no scratch outs, no eraser marks. It should not be folded, or bent. This form is a representation of you on paper and it should be pleasing to the eye and easy to read.

Content

Before you begin filling out the employment application read it over. Carefully follow the directions. Print neatly using an erasable black or blue pen. Never leave any of the blocks blank. If a block does not apply to you write not applicable (N/A). The objective is to acknowledge that you read it, so the employer won't think you intentionally left it blank or just overlooked it. Use powerful action words to describe your skills and accomplishments. The use of action words will help make a good positive impression. Also, it can help paint a clear picture of what you can do for the employer.

Example of power word usage:
Do not say, or write on your application/résumé, "I finished the following jobs..." **Do** say or write, "My accomplishments are..."
(See sample word lists beginning on page 51.)

(Tip: If there is not enough space in a block, use a clean sheet of paper and continue your answer, being sure to list the block number your information applies to. Also be sure to attach the paper to your application.)

Validity

Never lie on the employment application. It is grounds for dismissal. When completing an employment application consider the big picture. Think in terms of what you did, how you did it, and what you accomplished as it relates to the job you are applying for. This mind-set will enable you to express in writing exactly what you want the employer to know about your skills and work experience. It will also help you conduct a successful interview.

You will be able to provide a clear picture to the employer of what you can do for them, based on your skills and past experiences.

Completing an employment application

Listed below are the common blocks found on most applications. Read carefully; under each block is a description of the importance of the question and how you should answer it.

Block 1 – Last Name, First Name, Middle Initial
Pay close attention to the order of the name block(s), the order often varies on employment applications.

Block 2 – Present Address
List the address where you receive mail.

Block 3 – City, State, and Zip Code
Spell correctly and don't forget to list the zip code.

Block 4 – Today's Date
If you are submitting the employment application immediately following the completion, list the present date. But, if you take the application home to complete, list the date you will submit it.

Block 5 - Home Telephone Number

List the telephone number where you will receive your messages. Make sure the area code is listed. If you have your own telephone line, like most young people do when looking for a job, make sure your answering machine message is professional. Get rid of the long messages, the radical music, and the vulgar language.

Block 6 - Social Security Number

Always have your social security card with you for filling out applications and available as proof: your social security number is used all of your life to keep track of your medical care and employment taxes paid into the social security system, so that when you retire or become disabled or eligible for recipient death benefits you get the correct amount due to you. So, *do not guess*, make certain the number is correct.

Block 7 - Position Applied

Use the job title the employer used or what is listed on the source you are responding to, i.e., a job announcement, newspaper ad, bulletin.

Block 8 - Pay Expected

List "open" or "negotiable," unless you are familiar with the salary range or wages paid for that job. Be realistic. Don't price yourself out of the market, know the value of your skills, and what employers are paying for them.

Block 9 - Have you ever worked with us before?

Be honest. This is an opportunity for the employer to gather some history on you, to find out whether or not you are worth hiring. Your previous job performance may be the deciding factor used to determine if you are worth hiring.

Block 10 - Date available for work?

List "immediately" or an actual date. If you have a current employer make sure you give a two-week notice.

Block 11 - Hours available?

List only the hours you are available to work. If in doubt do not make yourself available. It will only cause more problems later for you and your employer.

Block 12 - Will you work overtime?

Consider your personal schedule. Know the time requirements for getting the job finished. But do remember that employers expect employees to be flexible.

Block 13 - How were you referred to us?

If you were referred by someone highly respected, list their name. They may give you a good reference. Otherwise, list how you heard about the job, i.e., friend, newspaper ad, sign, walk-in, etc.

Block 14 - Are you willing to travel?

Before answering this question consider your family and daily activities that may be affected by your decision. Specify your limits about traveling.

Block 15 - Do you have a valid driver's license?

If yes, list the state and expiration date. Identify the type of license you have. Example: auto

Block 16 - Are you a U.S. Citizen?

If not, list your employment authorization or alien resident card number that gives proof you are legally eligible to work in the U.S. If in doubt, contact the U.S. Immigration and Naturalization Department.

Block 17 – Do you have a physical condition which may limit your ability to perform the job for which you applied. If yes, describe:
Take precaution. If your physical limitations are not obvious you might want to wait until you get an interview before you reveal the condition. *Physical disabilities are considered only if they prevent you from performing the duties of the job.*

Block 18 – Person to notify in case of emergency:
List a reliable person. Someone who has daily contact with you. Example: parent, guardian, or close friend.

Block 19 – Education and Schools Attended:
Sr. High, Jr. High, and Grammar Schools
Spell out each school's name correctly. List current telephone and address. List all extracurricular activities that demonstrate your ability to lead and be a team player.

Block 20 – Employment History:
Do not use abbreviations. Include area code and current telephone numbers. Always show month and year using double digits. Use the number coding system (example: 01/00). Use "Mr. or Mrs." Be positive when listing your reason for leaving. Be descriptive and use power or action words. If you do not want the employer to contact your current employer briefly explain why.

Block 21– References:
For each of your references, list in the following order: first name, middle initial, and last name; current telephone number; address, including zip code.
(Tip: It is helpful if your reference works in the same industry.)

Sample of an employment application

Personal Information

Last Name [1]	First	Middle	Today's Date [4]
Present Address [2]			Home Phone [5]
City, State, Zip [3]			Social Security Number [6]

Job Information

Position Applied For [7]	Pay Expected [8]
Have you ever worked with us before? [9]	Date available for work. [10]

Hours Available [11]	Will you work overtime? [12]	How were you referred to us? [13]
Are you willing to travel? [14]	Do you have a valid driver's license? [15]	Are you a U.S. Citizen? [16]

Do you have a physical condition which may limit your ability to perform the job you are applying for? If yes, describe. [17]

Person to notify in case of emergency [18]	Phone

Education [19]

Schools Attended	# Yrs. Attended	City & State	Subjects Studied	Avg. Grades
Sr. High				
Jr. High				
Grammar				

List any memberships in professional or civic organizations

Employment History [20]

Company Name	Phone	Company Name	Phone
Address	Month/Yr. Employed	Address	Month/Yr. Employed
Name of Supervisor	Wage	Name of Supervisor	Wage
Job Title	Reason for Leaving	Job Title	Reason for Leaving
Duties		Duties	

May we contact your current supervisor?

References (list 3 people, not related to you, whom you have known at least 1 year) [21]

Name	Address	Position	Phone	Yrs. Known
Name	Address	Position	Phone	Yrs. Known
Name	Address	Position	Phone	Yrs. Known

Note:
Please feel free to practice with the complimentary application in the back of the book.

Verbs and power words

Use the action words below to fill out your employment application or résumé. Applications and résumés are tools used to introduce you to potential employers, so it is important to do a good job of writing them. It is best if the employers find your writing interesting to read. Using the wrong words or using a word too many times can give the reader a negative impression. It is worth taking the time to carefully construct your sentences. Your goal is to paint a creative picture of your "work self" by describing the way you work and giving the impression that you are a bright, hard working individual.

Helping skills are used with people to get the job done: (Words with an asterisk [*] are also communication skills.)

Words	Meanings
Accomplish	*Complete or get the job done*
Adjust	*Modify or change*
Advise*	*Give suggestions or information*
Attend *	*Show up or appear*
Care*	*Give concerned attention*
Direct*	*Provide management advice*
Guide*	*To lead*
Led*	*Took the lead*
Listen*	*Pay attention*
Mentor*	*Help guide someone*
Perceive*	*To understand*
Refer*	*Direct attention to*
Relate*	*To establish a connection*
Render*	*To give to another*
Service *	*To help or aid*
Speak*	*To express orally*
Teach	*Help someone learn*

Communication skills are used to communicate an idea or a point between two or more persons. They involve the qualities of listening, thinking, and speaking:

Words	Meanings
Arrange	*Group in an organized manner*
Conflict resolution	*Working with others to resolve controversy and disagreements*
Critical thinking	*Using sound judgment and reasoning*
Customer service	*Provide assistance*
Edit	*Rewrite, correct*
Negotiate	*To arrive at the settlement of some matter*
Persuade	*To influence another's thoughts*
Present	*Something presented*
Problem solve	*Find answers, solutions*
Proofread	*Check for errors*
Team-building	*Bring together*

Detail skills involve working with processes or things:

Words	Meanings
Approve	*Confirmation*
Arrange	*Put in order, prepare, or plan*
Classify	*Arrange according to class*
Collate	*Arrange in order*
Collect	*To gather together*
Compile	*To put together*
Dispatch	*To send out*
Enforce	*To strengthen*
Execute	*To perform tasks according to instructions*
Facilitate	*To help bring about*
Implement	*To carry out*
Inspect	*To view closely*

Judge	*To form an opinion*
Operate	*To work*
Organize	*To arrange systematically*
Record	*To track*
Retrieve	*To recover or regain*
Tabulate	*To count, record, or list systematically*
Validate	*To confirm or prove*

Teaching skills are used to explain ideas, processes, and information so others can understand and apply:

Words	Meanings
Adapt	*To adjust*
Advise	*To suggest*
Compare	*To match*
Contrast	*Degree of differences*
Develop	*To make better*
Dialect	*Manner of expressing oneself*
Evaluate	*To determine the worth or value*
Forecast	*To predict*
Interpret	*Explain or tell the meaning of*
Knowledge	*Being aware*
Plan	*A detail program*
Project	*To plan or estimate*
Research	*The collecting of information*
Teach	*To impart information*

Research skills are used to discover information:

Words	Meanings
Clarify	*Make easier to understand*
Collect	*To gather*
Critique	*To review*
Decide	*To make a decision*
Diagnose	*To recognize*

Gather	*To come together*
Interview	*To obtain information while conversing*
Investigate	*To closely examine*
Observe	*To take note of*
Recognize	*To admit or take notice of*
Review	*To view or see again*
Study	*To learn or memorize something*
Survey	*To examine as to condition, situation, or value*
Write	*To communicate by letter*

Management skills are used to plan, organize (manage), and coordinate people, activities, and projects:

Words	Meanings
Administer	*Conduct*
Analyze	*Study in detail*
Assign	*To appoint as a duty*
Contract	*Binding agreement between two or more*
Control	*To have influence over*
Coordinate	*To bring into a common action*
Delegate	*To assign responsibility or authority to*
Direct	*Determine a course or direction*
Hire	*To employ*
Initiate	*To begin something*
Prioritize	*To rank in order*
Perform	*To carry out*
Produce	*To bring about*
Recommend	*To present as worthy*
Schedule	*To designate a fixed time*
Supervise	*To oversee*
Terminate	*To end*

Technical skills are used to perform complex tasks and to troubleshoot:

Words	Meanings
Assemble	*Bring together*
Communicate	*To make known*
Enable	*To provide the means*
Encourage	*To inspire*
Inform	*To communicate knowledge*
Instruct	*To give an order*
Stimulate	*To activate*

Financial skills are used to communicate monetary issues, problems, and solutions:

Words	Meanings
Allocate	*To assign*
Audit	*To check*
Bill	*An itemized list*
Budget	*To set aside money*
Calculate	*To determine by mathematical process*
Compute	*To figure*
Decrease	*To reduce*
Detail	*Extended attention*
Increase	*To add*
Inventory	*Itemized list of assets*
Maintain	*To keep*
Purchase	*To buy*
Solve	*To answer*

Manual skills are used to assemble and breakdown equipment following specific guidelines and regulations:

Words	Meanings
Bend	*To curve*
Bind	*To constrain*
Build	*To construct*
Drill	*To make holes*
Handle	*Have a grasp on the situation*
Lift	*To elevate*
Move	*To motion*
Operate	*To run*
Pull	*To draw*
Punch	*To stroke*

Creative skills are used to find solutions to problems or needs that are cost-effective and also used to improve performance, generate ideas, or uncover hidden opportunities in problems:

Words	Meanings
Alter	*To change*
Ask	*To inquire*
Change	*To shift*
Create	*To originate*
Design	*To make an arrangement*
Generalize	*To make broad*
Listen	*To hear*
Modify	*To change*
Paraphrase	*To repeat*
Predict	*To guess*
Question	*To inquire*
Rearrange	*To sort*
Reconstruct	*To make over*
Regroup	*To reform*

Rename	*Change name*
Reorganize	*To redo*
Reorder	*To sort out*
Restate	*To reaffirm*
Revise	*To rework*
Rewrite	*To rephrase*
Simplify	*To make things easier*
Systematic	*Orderly*
Vary	*To differ*

Problem solving skills are used to determine the cause, define the improvement opportunity, develop solutions and execute a plan. It is most effective when input and critical comments are solicited from all:

Words	Meanings
Analyze	*To study in details*
Appraise	*To estimate*
Combine	*To put together*
Conclude	*To terminate*
Contrast	*A disagreement*
Criticize	*To speak negatively of*
Decide	*To conclude*
Derive	*To evolve*
Determine	*To come to a decision*
Diagnose	*To make out*
Formulate	*To draft*
Generate	*To originate*
Induce	*To bring about*
Infer	*To reason*
Regroup	*To reform*
Rename	*Change name*
Reorganize	*To redo*
Reorder	*To sort out*

Restate	*To reaffirm*
Revise	*To rework*
Rewrite	*To rephrase*
Simplify	*To make things easier*
Systematic	*Orderly*
Vary	*To differ*

Discriminative skills are used to determine the differences, strengths, and shortcomings of situations:

Words	Meanings
Choose	*To make a selection*
Collect	*Gather together*
Define	*To make distinct, clear or detailed*
Describe	*To represent or give an account in words*
Detect	*To discover or determine the existence, presence, or fact*
Differentiate	*To become distinct or different in character*
Discriminate	*To make a distinction*
Distinguish	*To make as separate*
Estimate	*To judge tentatively or approximately the value, worth, or significance of*
Identify	*The distinguishing character or personality of an individual*
Isolate	*Being alone*
List	*Simple series of words or numbers*
Locate	*To set or establish in a particular spot*
Match	*A pair suitably associated*
Omit	*To leave out*
Order	*The arrangement or sequence of objects*
Pick	*To select with care*

Place	*To appoint to a position*
Recognize	*Acknowledge acquaintance with*
Select	*Chosen from a number or group by fitness or preference*
Separate	*To set or keep apart*

Laboratory skills are used in a learning environment:

Words	Meanings
Apply	*To put to use for some practical purpose*
Calibrate	*To adjust precisely for a particular function*
Compute	*To make calculation*
Conduct	*To direct the performance of*
Connect	*To become joined*
Convert	*To change from one form or function to another*
Demonstrate	*To show or prove the value of*
Feed	*To give food to*
Grow	*To increase in size*
Insert	*To put or thrust in*
Keep	*To stay in accord with*
Lengthen	*A measure distance or dimension*
Limit	*Something that has a boundary, restrains, or confines*
Manipulate	*To manage or utilize skillfully*
Plant	*fit in place*
Prepare	*To get ready*
Remove	*To change the location position, station, or residence of*
Replace	*To put something new in the place of*
Report	*Detailed account or statement*
Reset	*To change the reading*

Set	*Fix by authority or appointment*
Specify	*To name or state explicitly or in detail*
Straighten	*To make straight*
Time	*The point or period when something occurs*
Transfer	*To convey from one person, place, or situation to another*
Use	*The method or manner of employing or applying something*
Weigh	*To consider carefully*

Computer language skills are used when talking about computers and related subjects:

Words	Meanings
Internet providers	*America On-line, Prodigy, etc., are nationally known; however, there are usually several in each local area*
Chat groups or rooms	*IRC (Internet Relay Chat). Internet on-line discussion between two or more people on-line and communicating together at the same time*
Databases/ spreadsheets	*Programs used to organize and to enter data, such as accounting or filing information*
Download/up-load	*Receiving or sending data over the Internet*
DTP (Desktop publishing)	*PageMaker, Microsoft Publisher, etc., programs used to create newsletters, magazines, books, flyers, etc.; all do typesetting and editing of text and graphics*
Computer programming	*Creating programs to be used in a universal computer format*

Electronic mail (E-mail)	*Communicating and sending messages locally or across the world over a phone line connected to a computer*
FTP (File Transfer Protocol)	*File libraries or archives available to the public*
Graphic/art programs	*CorelDraw, Adobe PhotoShop, etc.; used to create art in various forms*
Hardware	*Monitor, keyboard, printer, mouse, etc.*
Hypertext (HTML)	*The programming language used on the World Wide Web (WWW)*
Internet	*Some of the most common uses are e-mail; IRC (Chat); WWW; FTP file transfer protocol; conferencing (Net-meeting); news-groups (usenet)*
Presentation programs	*PowerPoint, HyperStudio, etc., are used to create a computerized visual presentation of a particular subject*
Search engines	*On the Internet: Yahoo, Alta Vista, Lycos, WebCrawler, etc.*
Software	*All computer programming, including the Microsoft Windows environment*
Websites	*Individual sites presenting information to anyone who 'visits' them — usually one site opens links to many others*
World Wide Web (www)	*A linking of web pages referred to as addresses or URLs*
Word processing programs	*Microsoft Word, Word Perfect, etc., are used to typeset and edit text and used to do desktop publishing*

Application tips

When completing employment applications on the spot, keep track of your time and speed. Have your social security number and current telephone numbers and addresses available. Write neatly and make certain all spelling is correct. To ensure the best results complete the sample résumé in this chapter before you venture out to an employer. It can be used as a guide. That way all of your information will be current and accurate, and you will not be guessing.

So, begin gathering all the information you're going to need for the completion of your practice application and don't forget to review the power word listings to help you. A properly prepared and completed employment application will open doors to unlimited opportunities for you.

Remember, to look for a job *alone.* Don't take your friends or relatives. Be prepared, carry a black pen with eraser; avoid embarrassment by knowing the present date; and dress appropriately.

You can do it!

So, now that you have been given the tools to obtain the job of your choice, put those skills to use and go forth to conquer that first job which is going to lead you straight to your dream career.

Good luck!

*Employment applications
are vehicles used to get an employer's attention:
if used creatively, unlimited opportunities will avail...*

Chapter 4
Résumés

Bill

Chapter 4
Résumés

Overview

What is a résumé? It is a document summarizing your high school courses, grades, academic and community honors, extracurricular and sport activities, paid and unpaid work experience, and specific skills that will give you the edge over your competition.

The résumé and employment application have similar purposes. Both may be used to apply for employment. Most likely, early in your job search the employment application will be the more requested of the two. But, as you advance in your job search, you will find the résumé to be the most preferred. The résumé *and* the employment application, will become your most valued tools for introducing your particular skills, abilities, accomplishments, and interests to a potential employer.

It would be a very good idea to prepare a résumé before you begin looking for work. Keep in mind that it will not replace the employment application, but having it on hand as a guide will make completing an application much easier since your information will be organized and well thought out in advance on the résumé. Also, being a student with a résumé gives the employer the impression that you are a very well-prepared person and have the potential to become a professional and someone well worth hiring.

There are many ways to write a résumé, however, the best way is to use the one that represents you well. If you are comfortable with the résumé you wrote, you will feel more confident in your job search.

So, although there is no *one* correct way to write a résumé, there are strategies you can use to best promote your "work-self" that will best get an employer's attention. The most creative aspect of résumé writing is selecting your format. The format you select should depend on your targeted audience and the manner in which you want to present yourself.

There are three basic types of résumés: *chronological, functional,* and *combination.* Each have particular features of their own and if used appropriately will serve to complement your professionalism, work experience, skills, and interests. In short, your résumé is your marketing tool to getting the employer's attention.

Therefore, you should carefully consider your circumstances before selecting your résumé format. Selecting the appropriate format will increase your chances of obtaining an interview. For instance, students using education instead of experience to qualify for a job may write a *functional* résumé, utilizing *functional categories* to describe and organize their skills and background rather than focusing on employment history. In this situation the functional resume will strengthen the student's position. The student is placing more value on education than work history, since he/she lacks direct work experience. The use of functional categories to creatively describe their work experience and skills will present them more favorably to the employer.

The first step in creating your résumé is to determine which jobs you are both qualified for and interested in. In today's job market it is *crucial* to be specific. If you are not sure about the type of work you are interested in, just review the results of your self-assessment. If you did not take a self-assessment, think deeply about your likes and dislikes. Consider your skills; you probably have a wide variety of skills that may be used in many different jobs. It's important to identify the skills you enjoy using the most and match them to a job. Review the *Dictionary of Occupational Titles, the Occupational Outlook Handbook,* want ads, information you have gathered at Career Fairs, and received from your networking contacts to help you identify the type of job you are interested in and capable of pursuing. After identifying the type of work you want to do, you need to select the résumé format that will best introduce you to employers.

In this chapter we will discuss the different techniques of résumé writing and give examples of the three basic types of résumés. As a general rule when writing your résumé you should include what relates to the job you are applying for and what demonstrates your ability to do the job.

Let's begin

Your résumé is a reflection of you

The résumé is your promotional piece. Use it as your calling card for introducing your unique skills and experience. Accompanied by a cover letter, its purpose is to get you an interview. Résumé writing is not an exact science. Suggestions and examples that appear in this chapter are merely general guidelines, not a blueprint.

Getting started

Writing your résumé requires a lot of thinking. You should start by listing your high school courses, grades, academic and community honors, extracurricular and sport activities, paid and unpaid work experience, and unique skills you enjoy using. Don't leave anything out at this point. Write down whatever comes to mind. This is called "brainstorming" and is referred to as your *career profile.* For accuracy you should review certificates, awards, report cards, position descriptions, school transcripts, and any other documents obtaining valuable information about your background, such as dates, grades, titles, and names. Then list them in order of importance and dates. This *organizing* of information will help when you decide where to place the items in your résumé.

Once your career profile is compiled and completed you are ready to begin writing your résumé. Begin by describing your experiences and use action words to communicate your skills. Use the top third of the page to get the reader's attention. List the most important and related responsibilities first, meaning those things that are directly related to the job you are applying for. Example: Highlights of Qualification is located at the top of the page, (if you choose to list this heading) in that category you would list the items you feel will give you the competitive edge; such as, special training, proficiency in a particular area, or having a security clearance, etc.

Your headings

Your personal heading is located at the top of the page. It should include: your name, address, telephone number, and e-mail address. Always use your business or official name, avoid nicknames. To reserve space list only one telephone number and address.

Your career objective

This is an optional section, but it is highly recommended. It tells the employer immediately what type of work you are looking for. Your objective should be employer-centered, clear, and concise. If you know the exact job title used by the employer, list it.

Examples of objectives are:
☆ A Cashier Position
☆ Cashier position requiring sales, customer service, and accounts payable/receivable skills.
☆ Position as a Cashier for Sears Roebuck and Co.

Your work experience

Usually the work experience area is next on your résumé. However, there are a few exceptions, but the rule-of- thumb is to list your education before your work history, because some employers view education as more valuable than work experience.

This section or major heading may be titled many different ways. You may list it as your *Work Experience, Employment Information,* or *Summary of Relevant Skills and Experience.* It depends on your preference and particular situation.

Your training

This is an optional section. If you have completed some type of formal training that is directly related to the position you are applying for, then include it on your résumé.

Your education

This category is particularly important if you are expecting educational experience to qualify you for the job. You want to list your major field of studies, grade point average (GPA), and any courses that are directly related to the field of work you are applying for.

Examples:
    East High School - Peaceful, Ohio 67892
    Major: Vocational Studies; GPA.: 3.0
    Related Courses: Accounting I & II; Grade: A
    Business Math; Grade: A

Courses:
If you list specific courses make sure they are related to the job or field you are applying for. The courses should be important to the employer's business or show a special academic focus.

GPA:
Some employers are very interested in your grades, while others are not. Deciding whether or not to include your GPA will depend on your past performance. Keep in mind that you should always present your accomplishments in the best possible light. Your GPA is an educational accomplishment. There isn't a rule saying that only your overall GPA can be placed on your résumé. Feel free to list your GPA in different ways if it improves your presentation. Just be sure to mention how you came to your conclusion.

Example:
    GPA: 3.0 in general studies
    GPA: 3.5 /4.0 previous semester

Your work history

In this area include date, position title, and the employer's name and location for each job held. List your current or most recent job first and work backwards from there.

Example:
Jan. 2002 -   Cashier, ABC Co., 12345 Friendly Lane
Present   Peaceful, Ohio 67890

Jan. 2001 - 2002   ABC Market, 222 Hillsdale
Jan. 2000 - 2001   Peaceful, Ohio 67890

Optional heading

The next few listed categories are optional headings you could use to make your résumé more appealing.

<u>Highlights of Qualifications:</u>
This one is used to share personal and professional traits you believe will make you a better candidate for the job. Normally three to five bullet statements are listed here. List only those things you believe will make you stand apart from your competition.

Example:
    Fluent in Spanish and French
    Proficient in using Point of Sales terminals
    Excellent communication skills
    Able to persuade and influence people to take action.

<u>Honors and Awards:</u>
Do not list your triumphs. It is better to select honors and awards which present a complete picture of your strengths rather than to list your triumphs. However, if you have had successes in extracurricular activities which demonstrate your many abilities, you may consider including them.

Choosing a format

When you select a résumé format, it is important to select the one that will show you off to the employer. Your selection will depend upon your experience, career goals, and previous accomplishments. The following pages contain descriptions and samples of three basic types of résumés.

The chronological résumé

The chronological résumé is the more traditional structure and most familiar to employers. The experience section is the focus of the résumé. You begin by listing your current or most recent job first. List the job title, give a detailed description of your duties and responsibilities, and list the company name and address. This structure is primarily used when you remain in the same type of work. It shows advancement in the career field and impressive titles of previous jobs. It communicates directly to the employer your purpose, past achievements, and probable future performance. This format will not work well for individuals who are looking for their first job, nor anyone with a patchy work history, which includes changing jobs or career fields frequently.

The advantages

The chronological résumé may appeal to older, more traditional readers and is best used for conservative fields. It is easier to see what you did in your jobs. It may help if the name of the employer stands out, but only if it is an impressive company.

The chronological résumé format:
☆   Is easy to read.
☆   Showcases growth in skills and responsibility.
☆   Shows promotions and impressive job titles.
☆   Shows company loyalty.

The disadvantages

It can be quite difficult to highlight what you do best. This format is rarely appropriate for someone making a career change or looking to enter into a new career field.

It can:
☆   Emphasize gaps in employment.
☆   Highlight frequent job changes.
☆   Emphasize employment, but not skill development.
☆   Emphasize lack of related experiences and career changes.
☆   Point out demotions and career setbacks.

Best used by
☆   Students with a steady work record.
☆   Students with experience that relates directly to the position they are applying for.

This style is designed to provide a comprehensive summary of your work history, education, and accomplishments.

Note:
Sample of the <u>chronological résumé</u> is on the following page.

Sophia Morris
123 FriendshipDrive
Peaceful, Ohio 45678
E-Mail Address: morris@aol.com
(000) 111-1111

Objective:	A Cashier Position
Education:	East High School, Peaceful, Ohio 45679 Major: Vocational Sales G.P.A.: 3.0

Work Experience:

Jan 2002-Present

Cashier
ABC Company, 12345 Friendly Lane
Peaceful, Ohio 67890
Greet and assist customers. Process cash, checks, and credit card charge transactions. Count money to verify amounts and issue receipts for funds received. Issue change and process checks for purchases. Compare totals cash register receipts with the amount of currency in register to verify balances.

Jan 2001-Jan 2002

Cash Clerk
DEF Company, 6789 Associate Drive
Peaceful, Ohio 67891
Received cash from customers or employees in payment for purchases. Made change, cashed checks, and issued receipts or tickets to customers. Read and recorded totals amounts shown on cash register tape and verified against cash on hand. Received and prepared reports of transactions.

Special Activities:

Jan 2002 - Present

Class President and active member of Vocational Sales Club

The functional résumé

The functional résumé highlights and organizes your skills, accomplishments, interests, and strengths to support your objective by using functional areas. It groups all of your work experiences into categories. The functional résumé format enables the reader to see immediately what you can do without reading the entire résumé. The reader has the luxury to scan over the résumé by reviewing the categories listed. Immediately, it can tell the employer whether or not you have the skills or experience he is looking for.

The advantages

The functional résumé will help you most in reaching for a new career goal or direction. This format is highly recommended for students with minimum skills who are looking for their first job. It supports the idea of using your educational experience or skills learned through unpaid work to qualify you for the job.

The functional résumé format:

☆   Emphasizes skills rather than work history; it allows the writer to focus on relevant experience.
☆   Organizes a variety of experience (paid and unpaid, and other activities).
☆   Disguises gaps in work history or a series of short-term jobs.
☆   Covers lack of progression.
☆   Is easy to read; easier to keep the length to one page.
☆   Is easier to *target* the résumé (relate your experience to the job).

The disadvantages

It does not reveal what the applicant did in each job, which may be negative to some conservative interviewers.

It can:

☆ Be viewed with suspicion by employers due to lack of information about specific employers and dates.

☆ De-emphasizes growth/job titles. Does not connect skills/accomplishments to specific work situations in the case of multiple employment.

☆ Require extensive background work or knowledge of job/employer.

☆ Need strong related work experience and/or skills.

Best used by:

☆ Students with no previous work experience.

☆ Students with gaps in employment.

☆ Students who have developed skills from volunteer and unpaid work experiences.

☆ Frequent job changes.

Note:
Sample of the <u>functional résumé</u> is on the following page.

Nikki Jones
123 Friendship Drive
Peaceful, Ohio 45678
Telephone Number: (000) 111-1111
E-mail Address: nikki@aol.com

- -

Objective:
A Cashier position requiring sales, customer service, and accounts payable/receivable skills.

Sales
- Sold men's and boys' outer garments, such as, suits, pants, and coats.
- Advised customer of styles and appropriateness of garments for particular occasions.
- Operated cash register to complete sales transactions. Opened and closed cash drawers. Balanced daily cash transactions.

Customer Service
- Greeted and assisted customers.
- Researched customer complaints and conducted follow-up.
- Advised customers of current sales and promotional opportunities.
- Referred customer to appropriate sources for assistance.

Accounts Payable/Receivable
- Compiled and posted in general ledgers.
- Calculated interest and added charges.
- Reconciled and balanced accounts.

Education: East High School,
Peaceful, Ohio 45679
Major: Vocational Studies
G.P.A.: 3.0
Related Courses:
Accounting I & II Grade: A
Business Math Grade: A

Special Honors and Activities:
Recipient of 'Chamber of Commerce Youth Business Award.'
Served as Distributive Educational Secretary for Class of 2001.

The combination résumé

The combination résumé includes elements of both the chronological and the functional formats. This format may be exactly what you need if you are a student looking to enter into a new career field with minimum transferable skills hoping to qualify for the job. You should stress your accomplishments and skills, and include your work history. It is not necessary to include dates unless they enhance your résumé. This is the perfect résumé for someone with work experience that wishes to change to a job in a related career field, or a student looking for education and work experience to qualify them for the job.

The advantages

The combination résumé maximizes the advantages of both kinds of résumés, chronological and functional.

It will:

☆ Highlight most relevant skills and accomplishments.
☆ De-emphasize employment history in less relevant jobs.
☆ Combine skills developed in a variety of jobs or other activities.
☆ Minimize drawbacks such as employment gaps and absence of directly related experience.

The disadvantages

They tend to be longer résumés. Shared information could be repetitious if listed in both the functional areas and work history section. It is best not to list detail description in the work history section. Only the basic information is needed to let the reader know where you previously worked, such as, the job title, company name, address, and dates employed.

It can:

☆ Be confusing if not well organized.
☆ Require more effort and creativity to prepare.

Best used by:

☆ Students looking for both education and work experience to qualify them for the job.
☆ Students who want to emphasize personal qualities, such as, initiative, dependability, and the ability to grow with a job.
☆ Career changers or those in transition.

Note:
Sample of the <u>combination résumé</u> is on the following page.

David Vernon
123 Friendship Drive
Peaceful, Ohio 45678
Telephone Number: (000) 111-1111
E-mail Address: vernon@aol.com

- -

Objective	A Cashier position requiring sales, customer service, and accounts payable/receivable skills.
Education	East High School, Peaceful, Ohio 45679 Major: Vocational Studies G.P.A.: 3.0 Related Courses: Accounting I & II Grade: A Business Math Grade: A

Highlights of Qualifications

- Fluent in speaking Spanish and French.
- Proficient in using Point Of Sales (POS) terminals.
- Knowledgeable of accounts payable/receivable postings techniques.
- Able to work with a diverse group of people.

Sales

- Sold outer garments for men and boys; such as, suits, pants, and coats.
- Advised customers of styles, and appropriateness of garments for par-ticular occasions.
- Operated the cash register to complete sales transactions. Opened and closed cash drawers. Balanced daily cash transactions.

Customer Service

- Greeted and assisted customers.
- Researched customer complaints and conducted follow-up. Advised customers of current sales and promotional opportunities.
- Referred customers to appropriate sources for assistance.
- Accounts payable and accounts receivable.
- Calculated and posted in general ledgers.
- Computed interest and added charges.
- Reconciled and balanced accounts.

Work History

Cashier	ABC Company 12345 Friendly Lane Peaceful, Ohio 67890	Jan 2002 - Present
Cash Clerk	DEF Company 6789 Associate Drive Peaceful, Ohio 67891	Jan 2001 - Jan 2002

Résumé guidelines

The following are general guidelines for writing your résumé. This information changes geographically and varies according to the person, situation, and profession.

The résumé format

☆ Length should be limited to one page, but never exceed two pages.

☆ Make margins (top, bottom, left, and right) approximately one inch.

☆ There should be plenty of white space and it should be easy to read: 50 percent white space and 50 percent print.

☆ Font size should be no larger than 12 point, but no smaller than 10 point. Use conservative font styles, such as Times New Roman, Helvetica, or Arial.

☆ Use black ink and/or fonts that are easy to read.

☆ Layout should be easy to follow and information should be easy to locate.

☆ Appearance should be neat and clean, no errors or corrections.

☆ Weight of paper should be 20- to 25-pound bond, rag or linen, and a neutral color.

☆ Envelope and cover-letter paper should match résumé paper.

☆ Align all justification to the left. Dates should also be left justified.

Résumé content

★ Show responsibility and results that relate to the needs of the company.

★ Give examples of accomplishments and the ability to solve problems.

★ Show statistics and numbers.

★ Be honest, positive, and specific.

★ Use category headings: objective, work experience, education, training, honors and awards. This will make your résumé more pleasing to read.

★ Avoid being wordy and using abbreviations. Use action verbs and be brief for greater impact.

★ Include volunteer experience, language, internships, and certificates that relate to the position.

★ Research the company and know what information would impress them.

★ Use industry terminology.

★ Be accurate with your information, make sure you use correct spelling and grammar.

General tips

★ Write your own résumé. Start by writing down a list of everything you've done, your work history, education, and all your accomplishments. Don't use a résumé writing service. It's costly, and they usually appear to be *too slick*; too prepared for sincerity.

★ Do not mass mail résumés. It is the worst thing you can do.

★ Résumés help you prepare what you want to say during the interview.

☆ Use a computer or type your résumé. Try copy centers, libraries, schools, or check with local job service centers to find out who has equipment to do résumés.

☆ Your résumé should be written to match the job you applied for.

☆ Take extra copies of your résumé; it is possible you could interview with other people.

☆ Some occupations don't need résumés. But it is always good to have it with you.

☆ Never provide names of references on your résumé. Either enclose a reference sheet or provide references when requested.

Writing a cover letter

The cover letter plays an important role in the job search process. If done properly it can increase your chances of getting an interview and strengthen your ability to compete for jobs. It adds a personal touch to your résumé and shows employers that you are a serious and professional applicant. A well-written cover letter demonstrates your communication and organizational skills and shows that you are the type of person who is willing to go the extra mile. In this highly competitive job market, the cover letter gives you a much needed edge over other applicants and allows you to describe how your specific skills and accomplishments uniquely qualify you for the job.

Three basic techniques for writing a cover letter

1. Tailor it to fit the employer's requirements: Before you start the writing process review the criteria for the position and make a list of what the employer wants. It may include specific areas of expertise, technical knowledge, transferable skills, and/or personality traits. Put those items in your letter to demonstrate that you have the desired qualifications and creatively describe how you can meet his needs.

2. Market yourself: Tell the employer why you should be hired. Be assertive about your qualifications, but don't be egotistic. The tone of your letter should be professional, yet personable. One of the best ways to judge your letter is to read it out loud. Make sure it's easy to read and you aren't tripping over your words. Work on it until it flows naturally and has a conversational tone.

3. Keep it simple: There are many ways you can prepare the format of this letter. If you are totally unsure review business books or get advice from a business teacher. It is recommended that you form the letter as a business letter. Use the simple block format with left flush margins (refer to the sample letter on Page 92). Limit it to one page, preferably three-to-five paragraphs with one-inch margins all around.

Letter content

<u>First Paragraph</u>: This is your introduction paragraph. Your objective is to get the reader's attention and describe the position you're interested in.

Example:
In response to your advertisement posted in the front window for a cashier position, I have enclosed my résumé for your review.

— or —

Your recent advertisement for a cashier's position caught my attention, as my qualifications appear to be very compatible with your requirements.

— or —

I was referred by...

Second Paragraph: This paragraph is the body of your cover letter. You should outline your qualifications for the position, those that make you the best candidate for the job. Focus on the most relevant aspects of your background, such as, experience, course work, grade-point average, and your personal and professional traits. Do not repeat what is in your résumé. You want to include information that will catch their attention and make them want to read your résumé.

Example:
My progressive two years of retail experience qualifies me as the best candidate for your position. As specified in your ad, I am skilled in sales, customer service, and accounting. In addition, I am the current recipient of the 'YMCA Youth Community Award.' After reviewing my résumé you will see my qualifications are a perfect match for your cashier position.

— or —

My qualifications for the position include the completion of a two-year business course requirement at East High School in Peaceful, Ohio. I completed the course work with a GPA of 3.8 and currently hold the highest honor award titled 'Business Student of the Year.' I am skilled in sales, customer service, and accounting.

Third Paragraph: This is the closing paragraph. You should request a meeting or personal interview. Mention that you look forward to hearing from them. Tell how you can be reached. Thank them for taking time to consider your application.

Example:
I look forward to meeting with you to discuss my qualifications and your job opportunity in detail. I will call on
Monday, January 10, 2002, to schedule a convenient time
to meet with you. Thank you for your time.

— or —

I believe that I can make a positive contribution to the
ABC Company and look forward to discussing my capa-
bilities in detail. I am available for a personal interview at
your earliest convenience and may be reached after 5
p.m. at the telephone number or e-mail address listed on
my résumé. Thank you for your consideration.

Note:
Sample of a <u>cover letter</u> is on the following page.

January 5, 2002

B. Ball, Owner
Fine Food Store
5050 West Way
Peaceful, Ohio 56234

Dear Mr. Ball,

In response to your advertisement posted in the front window for a cashier's position I have enclosed my résumé for your review.

My qualifications for the position include the completion of a two-year business course requirement at East High School in Peaceful, Ohio. I completed the course work with a G.P.A. of 3.8 and currently hold the highest award title, such as "Business Student of the Year." I am skilled in sales, customer service, and accounting.

I look forward to meeting with you to discuss my qualifications and the opportunity to know your company in detail.

I will call on Monday, January 10, 2002, to schedule a convenient time to meet with you. Thank you for your time.

Sincerely,

David Vernon
123 Friendship Drive
Peaceful, Ohio 45678
(000) 111-1111

Preparing a reference sheet

First: Identify at least six people whom you know would speak positively about your character, work values, and ethics. Three of the six individuals should know you *very* well. They should be familiar with your long- and short-term career goals, knowledgeable of your educational aspirations, and aware of the progress you have made toward your goals. You will be using them as your personal references, so choose wisely. The other three individuals should be able to speak intelligently about your professional self. They should be aware of your career and educational experiences. They should be able to speak of your accomplishments and contributions made in the world of work, as well as your educational success.

Your references could include a trusted teacher or school administrator. Also, consider asking an employer who hired you through a vocational program such as: Vocational Sales, Vocational Tech, or Distributive Education.

In other words, anyone with a good reputation whom you know and trust could be a reference for you.

Second: Ask each of the individuals you chose if they feel they can give you a positive reference?

Third: Give them a copy of your résumé for their review and comments.

Fourth: Ask each of your references to review your résumé and encourage them to ask questions if they have any. You want to satisfy their curiosity so they can speak with total confidence if questioned by your prospective employer.

Fifth: Inform them of the positions you are applying for; as above, this will prepare them if questioned by the employer.

Sixth: Show your appreciation by sending a thank you note for their support. No matter how close a person is to you, the small gesture of a thank you will put a smile on their face and a warm place in their heart for you.

Example of Professional References

Ms. Marva Campbell
1814 Lovelane, Peaceful, Ohio 12345
(216) 795-4140
Job Title: Department Manager

Ms. Cathy Knight
360 Happiness Peak, Peaceful, Ohio 67890
(216) 421-1134
Job Title: Sales Supervisor

Mr. Giles Hudson
2722 Goodwill Ave., Peaceful, Ohio 01293
(216) 925-3709
Job Title: Accounting Unit Supervisor

Example of Personal References

Ms. Nancy Taylor
3704 Adventure Rd., Peaceful, Ohio 34567
(216) 441-3378

Mr. Richburg
732 Rhythm Rd., Peaceful, Ohio 67890
(216) 781-7766

*A teen with a résumé illuminates
confidence and professionalism...*

Chapter 5
Interviewing

Nikki

Chapter 5
Interviewing

Overview

This is quite different than the *informational interview* we discussed earlier in Chapter 2. There you interviewed people working at a particular job to see if you might also like such a position. Now, you will be preparing for an interview with a possible future employer.

Just what does the word *interview* mean? When you break the word down into its smallest parts: the first part, 'inter,' means *between*, and the second part, 'view,' means to *look at*. In this chapter the word interview has been defined by the author as "communication taking place between two people looking at each other." This is what should be going on during an interview. Both the interviewer and the interviewee should be exchanging information, and actively listening to one another.

Once you get to the interviewing phase of your job search, all of the hard work you put into your job search is about to pay off. To ensure success at this point we will discuss the interviewing process, effective strategies, and questions that may be asked during an interview.

The interviewing process

The interviewing process has four major parts. If you can clearly define each part and understand your role, as well as the employer's role in each part, you are on your way to landing that important job.

Part One - The Introduction
Your introduction is very critical. Employers form their *first impressions* at this stage. Within the first two-to-five minutes of an interview you are being sized up. You only get one chance to make a good first impression. And impressions seldom change during the remaining time of the interview. To guarantee yourself a good start and to make a positive first impression you want to be prepared.

The idea is to look your best. Arrive at least 15 minutes early. Be aware of your body language. Greet everyone you come in contact with politely and with a smile. Show enthusiasm and give a firm handshake.

Part Two - The Employer's Agenda
The employer's goal is to determine if your skills and abilities match the job, and identify whether or not you would fit into this company.

The employer needs more information about you. That is why employers interview. The employer's agenda is to find out as much as possible about you, so a decision to hire can be made. The employer wants to know your reason for wanting the job, how your skills and experience can help the company, whether you will fit in with others who are currently working for the company, and how much money you are going to cost them. Most likely, they will not ask you those questions directly. But they are trained and skilled in asking probing questions to get their answers.

It is your responsibility to be prepared to answer each question truthfully and with substance. Later in this chapter we will discuss questions asked during an interview.

Most importantly remember employers look for positive, "can-do" candidates who are self-starters, eager to accept a challenge.

Part Three - The Applicant's Agenda
It is your responsibility to tell the employer that you are interested in the job, company, and career field. Convince the employer that you are the best qualified candidate for the job. You want to help make the interview a dialogue rather than a one-sided conversation.

It is very important to ask questions. It shows you are interested in the job. Although it is best to limit your questions to four or five, if further clarification is needed, then go ahead and ask as many questions as needed to make certain the job is right for you. Remember, you are there to determine if *you* want to work for that company, if your skills match the job requirements, and to find out if there is growth potential for your future.

Be prepared by knowing what questions you are going to ask. Place your most important questions at the top of the list. Make sure all your questions are job related. Ask what the challenges of the position are, and confirm that you *understand the issues* before you tell how you can help solve them. Before the interview ends ask the employer if there are any questions or areas that he/she would like you to elaborate more on.

One exception: **do not** ask questions about salary or benefits until a job offer has been made. (Keep in mind why you are there and that you have the right to decline an offer.)

Part Four - The Closing
You want to thank the employer for his/her time. Ask about the next step in the interview process. If a second interview is required, ask who will be the interviewer and when you can expect a call. Or, if a second interview is not required ask when a decision will be made.

Get permission to call back to talk with the employer if you haven't heard from them by a specified date. Close the interview with a firm handshake and a positive up-beat statement.

Ask for a business card with the employer's name, telephone number, and address so you can send a thank you note to the right person with the correct information. When you send your thank you note handwrite it on quality paper and recap the main points of the interview. Keep it to half a page. In your note reflect the same positive attitude and enthusiasm shown at the interview.

Interviewing strategies

Your goal during the interview is to find out as much as you can about the job, while presenting yourself as positively as possible. Since good performance in the interview is essential to landing the job, you must learn how to keep the interview moving in the direction you want it to go. Candidates have the most success when they know themselves, what they want, and can relate it to the employer. During the interview, potential employers want to know if your interests, skills, values, salary requirements, and desired level of responsibility match what they have to offer. Either directly or indirectly, employers will ask (1) *Why are you there?* and (2) *What can you do for them?*

Research networking

Research the company to make a good impression. Employers want to meet candidates who have taken the time to learn about their company. You are demonstrating to the interviewer that you have a plan and are thorough. It will help you develop questions to ask during the interview about the industry, company, job, and employer. Your conversation during the interview will be smoother. The more you learn about the company the more you will have in common with the interviewer. It will increase your confidence level, and you will be able to make a more informed decision about the company. Your decision to work for a company should be based on your awareness of their strong and weak points. Research alone will not land you the job, but it will give you an advantage over other candidates. Research is what separates the organized applicant from those who are not prepared. It also ensures that you are not wasting your time pursuing companies in which you really have no interest.

People

Networking with people is one of the most important things you can do in your job search. Developing a network of people who can provide you with valuable information about prospective employers, opportunities, fresh leads, and encouragement will keep you a step ahead of your competition. You can begin your networking by talking with teachers, friends, relatives, and community leaders and letting them know that you are looking for employment. Share important information with them, such as, the type of employment you're interested in, the distance you're willing to travel, and when you are available.

Written materials

Review each company's written materials. Most employers try their best to represent themselves in print. Corporations, public and private agencies, and small businesses produce annual reports and newsletters about their operations. They are very eager and happy to provide this information to you because they regard such distribution as good relations with the public. If you ask for this information you will receive it.

You can find the names and addresses of companies from publications in your local library.

"Acing" the interview

Knowing exactly what you want and don't want to say during the interview will help you make a good impression. Think about what you want to say, write it down, and memorize your skills that are relevant to the job. An interview is a two-way communication exchange between an interviewer and interviewee. It involves both verbal and nonverbal communication. Focus on the content of what you will say and what your body language or nonverbal messages express. It is very important to understand the communication process that takes place during an interview. In order to conduct a successful interview, the interviewee must understand the significance behind each question asked. This section addresses what the interviewer is *really* trying to ask without being direct, and how intangible assets are identified and valued in the decision-making process.

Basically, there are four areas the interviewer focuses on to determine whether or not you are a match for the company and position.

First: The professional *you*: Will you be loyal, reliable, and trustworthy? This will reveal to the employer the degree of respect you will have for your job and the company.

Second: Your skills: Will they meet the requirements of the job?

Third: Your achievements/accomplishments: What you have done in the past is a good prediction of your future performance?

Fourth: The *personal* you: What type of person are you? How do you feel about yourself, and your chosen career? What would you be like to work with or around? The exchange of information should reflect the areas mentioned. Your answers to the employer's questions should be positive and emphasize your strengths not weaknesses. Remember, the interviewer also wants to know what your weaknesses are, they need to know why they should or shouldn't hire you for the sake of the business. When answering your questions, both the substance and the form of your answer should be positive. For example, words such as *couldn't, can't, won't,* and *don't* may create a negative tone and distract from the positive and enthusiastic image you want to display. During the interview you want to provide brief, to-the-point answers that relate your skills and experience to the needs of the company and employer. When possible, and if appropriate, the knowledge of the company you obtained through research and networking should be included in your answers.

You should practice for the interview by anticipating what questions might be asked and preparing your answers ahead of time. *Preparation* and *practice* are the key to doing your best. Most of the questions will relate to the following: educational background, related experience, career goals, personality, and related concerns.

Some of the most frequently asked questions include:
<u>Education</u>
☆ Describe your educational background.
☆ What is your major field of study?
☆ Why did you choose this field?
☆ What subjects did you enjoy the most? Why?

☆ What subjects did you enjoy the least? Why?
☆ Tell me about the best/worst teacher you ever had?
☆ What is your grade-point average?
☆ What leadership positions have you held?
☆ Why were your grades so low? Or why were your grades so high?
☆ What are your plans for furthering your education?
☆ What new skills do you hope to gain through education?
☆ If you could start your educational journey all over, what would you do different?
☆ Where do you want to be five years from now?

Work Experience (paid and nonpaid)

☆ What other jobs have you held?
☆ What were your major achievements in past jobs?
☆ What is your typical workday like?
☆ What skills do you enjoy using the most?
☆ What did you like about your boss?
☆ What did you dislike about your boss?
☆ Which job did you enjoy the most? Why?
☆ Which job did you least enjoy? Why?
☆ In order to fill this job, you must be bonded. Is there any problem that this presents?
☆ Tell me about a problem you could not solve?
☆ How would you describe your enemy?

Career Goals

☆ Why did you leave your last job?
☆ Why do you want to work for our company?
☆ Why do you think you are qualified for this position?
☆ Why are you looking for another job?
☆ Ideally, what would you like to do?
☆ Why should we hire you?

☆ How would you improve our operations?
☆ What do you want to be doing five years from now?
☆ What do you want to be earning five years from now?
☆ What are your short-term goals? (One year time frame)
☆ What are your long-term goals? (Two to five years)
☆ When will you be ready to begin work?
☆ What attracted you to our organization?
☆ How do you feel about working overtime?

Personality and Other Concerns

☆ Tell me about yourself?
☆ What are your major weaknesses?
☆ What are your major strengths?
☆ What causes you to lose your temper?
☆ Do you have any hobbies?
☆ What do you do in your spare time?
☆ What type of books do you read?
☆ What role does your family play in your career?
☆ How well do you work under pressure?
☆ When you have a deadline, how do you handle it?
☆ Are you a *self-starter*?
☆ What type of traits do you prefer in people you work with?
☆ How creative are you?
☆ If you could change your life, what would you do differently?

Remember to prepare your answers ahead of time. Put each question on an index card and have a friend or family member ask you the questions. This will give you the opportunity to practice out loud. You want to practice, practice, and practice some more until your responses flow naturally.

☆ Think before you speak.

☆ Respond intelligently to all questions.

☆ Effectively communicate your personal and professional traits. Balance yourself; sell your skills, experience and abilities, as well as your personality and attitude.

☆ During an interview do not talk about money unless the employer brings up the issue first. If unsure of the starting salary, just ask the employer what they will pay an individual with your skills and experience. Do not short yourself by agreeing to — or requesting — a salary before doing your research. Your ultimate goal is not to mention salary until an offer has been made. This is one reason why it is very important to do your research before you begin applying for employment.

Tips for preparing *thank you* letters

☆ Prepare your thank you letter in a business letter format.

☆ Address your letter to the person who interviewed you.

☆ Make certain you have the correct spelling of the interviewer's name, include title, organization, and complete mailing address.

☆ Express your appreciation for the interview, tour of the facilities, and the meeting of the employees.

☆ Re-emphasize your skills and qualifications that perfectly match the job and how the company can gain from them.

☆ Briefly include information you forgot to mention during your interview that is of upmost importance.

☆ Close by stating your future contact plans.

The body of your *thank you* letter

1. **Paragraph One:** Express appreciation for their time. Mention those things you were appreciative of: the tour of facilities, meeting the employees, overview of the company's purpose and future goals.

2. **Paragraph Two:** Re-emphasize your desire to work for the company. Tell how your skills perfectly match the job. Talk about the contributions you could make in that position.

3. **Paragraph Three:** Close with a sincere thank you and state your plans for the follow-up.

Note:
Sample of a <u>*thank you letter*</u> *is on the following page.*

January 6, 2002

B. Ball, Owner
Fine Food Store
5050 West Way
Peaceful, Ohio 56234

Dear Mr. Ball,

I appreciated the interview opportunity at Fine Food Store on Monday. The tour of the store and your overview of the store's setup and function gave me a clear understanding of the cashier's position. In particular, I was impressed with the state-of-the-art point of sales terminals and the quality of customer service you expect to be rendered.

The entire experience has confirmed my desire for employment as a cashier with Fine Food. My completion of a two-year business course has prepared me well for this position. Based on my interview, I know that I am a perfect candidate for the job and will fit in well with the Fine Food staff.

Again, thank you for the experience of getting to know your organization better. I look forward to hearing from you in the near future.

Sincerely,

David Vernon
123 Friendship Drive
Peaceful, Ohio 45678
(000) 111-1111

Actively listen and ask questions.
It is up to you to determine the fit between
your skills and the company's requirements,
which will help you make a good career decision
about each job you research into…

Chapter 6
The
Employer's Perspective

Chapter 6
The Employer's Perspective

Yes, come with us and we'll get started!

Bill   Sophia

Overview

The preceding chapters described how to conduct a successful "job search." You were introduced to **self-assessment tools,** learned how to **research** for helpful information and then how to complete an **employment application,** you were exposed to the basic formats of **résumé** writing, and taught how to conduct *win-win* **interviews.** Now it is time to put it all together! So, in this chapter we will review the **employer's perspective** and examine how the information you have studied will apply to you and the real world.

The "employer's perspective" is a direct result of a survey that 100 kind employers took their time to fill out and return to help you with your job search. Each of these employers work in a variety of career fields, ranging from the retail business to the food service.

They were required to meet the following criteria:

☆ Experienced in interviewing individuals aged 15 through 25.

☆ Had the authority to hire and fire individuals.

☆ Employed in a company or industry where the workforce was predominately between the ages of 15 and 25 years.

☆ Demonstrated a strong desire to work with young people and were interested in a young person's success.

We asked them to tell us in detail what they *liked* and *disliked* about working with this age group and then we carefully analyzed and grouped this information into the following three major categories:

☆ **The *do* lists.** What employers particularly value in the workplace and therefore what potential employees should attempt to *do* on their applications and during the interview.

☆ **The don't lists.** What employers felt potential employees should *not do* (*never do*) on their application, during an interview, or after being hired.

☆ **Words of wisdom** and **encouraging messages.** The participating employers jotted down many tips to support the success of young people like you who are entering the workforce for the first time.

A note about the "dos" and "don'ts" —

These dos and don'ts are listed in order of category and time frame. There is no order of *importance,* because these caring employers and this author feel that each listed **do** and **don't** is of *equal importance* for you to pay attention to.

The application and résumé *do* list:

Do...

1. ... be properly dressed when picking up an employment application or delivering a finished application.
2. ... have your résumé and reference sheets available.
3. ... write neatly or type your employment application.
4. ... fill in every line on the application, or at least acknowledge that you have read it by writing "nonapplicable" (N/A) in the block.
5. ... list your achievements and awards as they apply to the job or career field.
6. ... list all of your training experiences, i.e., certificates, such as, Red Cross certification, and/or other community certifications.
7. ... write a detailed description of your past work experiences using examples.

The interview *do* list:

Do...

1. ... be punctual; however, it is good practice to be early at least 15 minutes before your scheduled appointment. This shows your eagerness and interest.

    Note: If an emergency comes up, be considerate and responsible enough to call and explain the situation, then reschedule as soon as possible.

2. ... act maturely.
3. ... be particularly neat and appropriately dressed for your interview.
4. ... show good manners: stand up when you are approached by your potential employer and give a firm handshake; always be respectful.
5. ... know and use the employer's name correctly.
6. ... introduce yourself, if necessary.
7. ... be polite, speak clearly, and have direct eye contact with everyone you speak to.
8. ... be cheerful and show high energy, and be extremely outgoing to people.
9. ... have a positive attitude, and be prepared *to sell yourself.*
10. ... show confidence, be relaxed, and tell them what you are looking for.
11. ... use your *people skills.*
12. ... be flexible and open.
13. ... show a willingness to learn.
14. ... research the company and know what they do.
15. ... be current on industry trends and changes.

    (Refer to Chapter 2, as to how you can research this information).

16.   ... bring your youthful energy and exuberance to the business.
17.   ... show plans to stay with the company for a long period of time.
18.   ... state why you are the best person qualified for the job when asked, or given a suitable opening. Take the opportunity to state plainly that you want the job and will serve the company well.

The application *do not* list

These are reasons that may prevent you from being hired.

Do *not*...

1.   ... call a company and casually ask if they are hiring.
2.   ... yell at people in or outside of their place of business.
3.   ... use slang or vulgar language. *It is not acceptable in any business environment.*
4.   ... have inaccurate information on your form.
5.   ... hand in a torn or stained application.
6.   ... use a pencil to fill in an application.
7.   ... hand in a sloppily written application.
8.   ... use white out, or make scratch outs.
9.   ... make repetitive statements on your application or résumé.
10.   ... hand in an incomplete application.
11.   ... hand in an unsigned form.

The interview *do not list*

Do *not...*

1. ... be tardy; if you are not on time for the interview employers will rightly assume that you will most likely not show up for work on time.
2. ... bring friends to the interview, nor should you *ever* say that you must leave because someone is waiting for you.
3. ... have poor hygiene, i.e., be unshaven, have bad breath, a body odor, long, unkempt hair, or poor grooming habits (dirty nails, biting nails, chewing on your hair, etc.).
4. ... chew gum or have candy in your mouth.
5. ... display negative actions by dressing trendy and "street-like," i.e., shorts, tank tops, etc. It shows a lack of professionalism and inconsideration for the business and the potential employer.
6. ... show excessive nervousness, yet, on the flip side, try not to be too reserved either.
7. ... have poor body language, i.e., slouching, sitting on the edge of the chair, be stiff and unapproachable (*a chip on your shoulder*).
8. ... cross your arms; this body language is known to show a negative attitude.
9. ... give simple *yes* or *no* answers during an interview, causing the employer to do all the talking.
10. ... mumble your answers, employers want you to be direct, clear spoken, and talkative.
11. ... use slang phrases such as, "you know," or "like," this is immature and disrespectful.
12. ... give long answers to questions, and do not be a "know it all" individual.

13.   ... be irresponsible, careless, or unfocused.
14.   ... repeat yourself.
15.   ... use expressions such as "um," which could mean that you are easily distracted, unsure, or just an impolite individual.
16.   ... leave your answers unfinished.
17.   ... jump to conclusions before a question or statement is voiced.
18.   ... interrupt during a conversation.
19.   ... elaborate on your negative qualities.
20.   ... show a lack of experience. They expect you to be ambitious and motivated, so you might share volunteer experiences or information where you provided assistance to your neighbors or community.
21.   ... *complain* about previous employers.
22.   ... give or speak of your poor personal outlook on life.
23.   ... hesitate to speak up and ask questions, it shows an indifference to the job and company, which of course means *the job is not your priority.*
24.   ... put your eyes on the floor (or ceiling, or somewhere else, which would be *away* from the person interviewing you). *Be careful to not give the impression that you are indifferent.*
25.   ... stare into space, it implies you are not interested, nor mature enough for the job.
26.   ... state that you are not impressed by the employer's company or organization.
27.   ... request time off before you start working.

The *do not* list after you are hired

Do *not*...

1. ... have excessive absences. The company rightfully expects you to be there on time as scheduled.
2. ... miss your work commitments to the company.
3. ... stand around being idle, (this is the time to be creative and find work to keep busy.)
4. ... complain, or gossip, or listen to the grapevine.
5. ... be playful or waste time.

Words of wisdom encouraging messages

Employers passed on the following **"words of wisdom"** and **"encouraging messages"** to teens looking for a job. We used each employer's exact wording so you will understand the true effect of their expectations.

1. "Dress for success when picking up and dropping off employment applications."
2. "Anything excessive is unattractive."
3. "If not hired by one employer, do not take it personally, keep going for what you want and what will make you happy."
4. "Be serious about whatever you are out to achieve."
5. "Stay focused, friendly, and reliable."
6 "When searching for a job always be prepared with transportation to make it to the interview.
7. Always remember to look and feel your best!" *(This is an attitude and it is within your control.)*
8. "Be yourself and let your personality shine through."
9. "Take classes to prepare yourself for the job search process."
10. "Relax, think positive, and be confident."
11. "Have a positive attitude and be confident."
12. "Do the best you can do at each job. Any previous job performances will affect future job opportunities. Don't be discouraged."
13. "Work hard! You'll move up in life."
14. "During the interview, sell yourself to the company."
15. "Eye contact is the key."
16. "Be persistent if you want to go after the job and always follow up."
17. "Appearance and attitude are very important."

18. "Be polite, smile a lot, and make yourself available to work. The more wide open your availability the more attractive you become."
19. "Be mature, don't be shy, and *do* look professional."
20. "Be persistent when looking for work. Be friendly and outgoing and make good eye contact. You'll often get put off or discouraged in your job search, do not take it personally. Most companies interview a lot of applicants just for *one* position."
21. "Sell yourself to the interviewer."
22. "Be positive, be professional, relax, do the best job, give 100 percent not 90 percent. Be aggressive and always remember to smile!"
23. "Educate yourself on the position you are applying for. Always make eye contact, speak clearly, and don't give one-word answers. Always back up your answers."
24. "If you are going to work for someone, be sure to give them your *all* and be prepared to learn. Remember that someday you will be in their position helping another young person."
25. "If you put in 110 percent all the time you can be confident you've tried your best."

Job search skills

Employer's were also requested to comment on three areas that are critical to the success of a job seeker: *communication skills, transferable skills,* and *body language.* These are the tips they gave that would contribute to conducting a successful job search.

Communication skills

1. Be an effective listener and pay attention.
2. Speak clearly and use examples or tell about the actual event when explaining your work experience.
3. Give direct answers and explain your actions.
4. Don't take your parents with you to look for a job and have them do the talking for you.
5. Be articulate, clearly communicate your ideas.
6. Be flexible. Be attentive to the person you are talking with. You do not talk to adults the same as you do your friends.
7. Use the proper pronunciation of words.
8. Speak to everyone with respect and listen to what they have to say.
9. Learn how to resolve conflicts and relate to others.
10. Be prepared to ask questions.
11. Use impressive words.
12. Be honest, polite, and do not use slang.
13. Be well spoken, talkative, and use good posture.

Transferable skills

1. Sports teach excellent team work.
2. Baby-sitting jobs and paper routes give a sense of responsibility.

3. Prior work experiences.
4. Able to listen, advise, and share with others are all great attributes of having people skills.
5. Tracking and record keeping shows that you have been responsible for your daily course schedules and staying on top of assignments.
6. Meeting deadlines: turning class assignments in on time.
7. Prior public relation experiences: Held a school office, or an active member of a respected club or organization (Scouts).
8. Pleasant personality and good attitude.
   9. Customer service: Having been in an elected position in school has aided you in knowing how to speak with people and therefore you should not have public relation problems in the workforce.
10. Computer lab experiences.
11. Salesmanship: Having spoken and presented ideas to your school's student body you are better prepared for the sales workforce.
12. Outgoing, enthusiastic, and friendly personality. Everything else can be taught.
13. The ability to work well with others.
14. Leadership: a dominant good people skill. An example is taking the lead in extracurricular activities.

Body language

1. Sit up straight. Don't squirm around in your seat.
2. Make good eye contact and try not to make nervous fidgeting movements.
3. Reach out confidently and give a firm handshake.
4. Should display confidence. It should appear that you deserve the job, not be overly humble about *wanting* or *needing* it.

5. Appear relaxed and at ease while talking with people you do not know.
6. Smile, keep eye contact, and sit up straight and still.
7. Avoid the excessive use of your hands when you talk.
8. Sit and look at the interviewer.
9. Do not cross your arms.
10. Do not have wandering eyes when being interviewed in a busy area.
11. Avoid slouching, biting nails, and sweating.
12. Ladies should pay close attention when crossing their legs. No one wants to see your underwear.
13. Maintain good posture.

After carefully reviewing the employer's expectations and comparing the information in the preceding chapters, it should be easier for you to identify and determine your course of action. Now, you should be able to effectively plan your career path and your job search should be fun. Just remember to be positive, friendly, and always smile. Try not to be nervous about interviewing, after all, it is merely a part of the process. And once you begin your interview, relax, speak clearly, and sit straight. If you do not understand something, remember that you can *ask questions*, and you should never assume *anything*.

Ladies dress nice, not trendy, nor slatternly. And gentlemen, you should also dress nicely and be neat. Everyone should use their cologne conservatively; you do not want the odor of your cologne to be distracting. Also be just as conservative with your jewelry: ladies and gentlemen alike, remove all facial rings (and gentlemen you should also remove your *ear*rings) as these rings are not acceptable in the workforce and are a safety factor while on many types of jobs. Remember, you want to be selected *because* of your skills and experience, *not rejected because of a fad that will not fit into what a company views as a presentable employee.*

Develop a plan and put it into action. Set goals and conquer them. Most importantly, remember to go alone when you look for a job; never bring others with you because *you* will not be taken seriously.

Inquiries about whether or not an employer is hiring must be done politely. And when given an interview date and time, be punctual, if possible even be a little early.

Smile and make direct eye contact. Show enthusiasm about wanting the job. Be aggressive, assertive, and adventurous.

After reading this book your confidence should increase many fold, and rumors and negative stories you've heard about the job search process should no longer have any value. Now you should be ready to go out and conquer that job.

*Be honest and positive, remember that
knowledge is power if shared, so take heed and
act upon the employer's shared words in this chapter...*

Chapter 7
Salary Negotiation

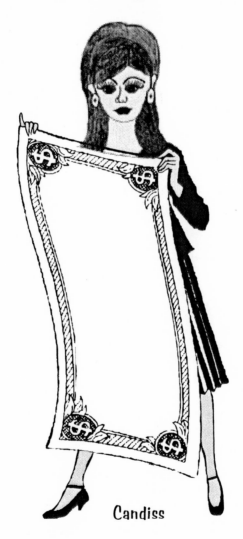

Candiss

Chapter 7
Salary Negotiation

Overview

As a teenager, at the beginning of your career journey,
the types of jobs acces-
sible to you will have non-
negotiable salaries and
wages. There is a direct re-
lationship between work
values and finances. Being
clear about what you ex-
pect and value in a job can
have a direct effect on how
much money you can make.
That is why it is so important to identify your values
as they relate to working.
Having a strong work ethic
and good work values can
provide opportunities that
may not otherwise be available to you. For instance, if
your work ethics include
any of the items listed on

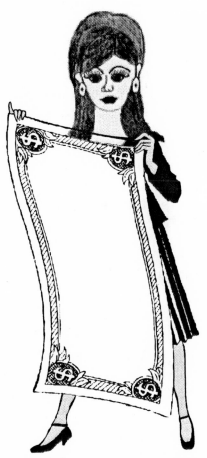

the following page, you will advance at a faster pace
than your counterparts. Also, these factors will strengthen
your position when requesting an increase in salary or
wages prior to the scheduled time.

Good ethical practices

1. Show up for work on time.
2. Strive for perfect attendance.
3. Perform with excellence.
4. Be responsible; carry out all assigned duties and responsibilities.
5. Aggressively seek out additional duties and responsibilities.
6. Willingly accept extra work assignments.
7. Provide outstanding customer services.
8. Approach your supervisor directly and ask what you can do to get promoted.
9. Obtain focus and remain focused.
10. Ask for help and clarification if you do not understand what is expected or what you should be doing.
11. Show interest in your job, and that you like what you are doing.
12. Share ideas on how to do the job more efficiently.
13. Foster healthy working relationships.
14. Address your concerns or issues in a positive way.

You will get promoted faster and be noticed as worthy of a promotion by doing the things listed above. Positive recognition will contribute to your success.

Know your work values

You should know what is important to you in a job. Being clear about what you value most within a job will help you decide whether or not the job is right for you, or if you should remain on that particular job.

Review the following checklist to determine what is most important to you in a job right now. Also, it is important for you to keep in mind that your work values will change over time due to differing circumstances in your life.

Current work values are important to you

(Place a check mark by the items most important to you)
____ Working as a team member
____ Opportunity to learn new things
____ Helping others
____ Environment fostering competition
____ Working environment "inside"
____ Working environment "outside"
____ Using your hands
____ Working with details, data, numbers
____ Working with *things* and machinery
____ Working alone
____ Working with people
____ Challenging and rewarding work
____ Good salary
____ Earning extra income
____ Performing a variety of tasks
____ Advancement opportunities on the job
____ Job recognition

_____ Routine work
_____ Bosses expectations clearly defined
_____ Persuading or influencing others
_____ Flexible work hours
_____ Set work schedule
_____ Freedom of expression
_____ Able to present and implement ideas
_____ Being a team member
_____ Creativity

When you search for a job keep these particular items in mind. Look for the job that will offer most of the items that are important to you.

Know your work and career values;
then go after what your heart dictates,
the success and money will eventually follow...

Chapter 8
If You Must Quit a Job

Bill

Chapter 8
If You Must Quit a Job

Overview

How to get out of a bad situation...
If you discover that a job is not right for you or perhaps your skills do not suit the workplace and tasks after you have committed yourself and begun working for a company, do not despair, there is a way out. *However, you do not quit a job by failing to show up for work.* There is a proper course of action to follow when you want to resign from a job. And you have a *moral* and *ethical duty* to follow this course, as we all do.

First of all, before you consider quitting, try to work things out. Identify the problems you find most unpleasant, and be *specific* in the process. I suggest you write down your

concerns in the order of importance. This will put things in a better perspective and is a very good reality check for your own peace of mind.

Then, once you have determined what the issues are, begin developing a plan of action. If appropriate, and the problems are not directly related to the supervisor, involve your supervisor, this is part of his or her job. Discuss your concerns openly *and* by all means be receptive to suggestions. Obtain clarification from your supervisor and sincerely attempt to reach a satisfying solution.

However, if the problem includes the supervisor, go to the company's Human Resource representative. Ask the representative to assure you that your name will remain anonymous and the conversation will be kept private. Then proceed to discuss your issues and ask for guidance. If it is impossible to work out your problems, *only then* should you consider it best to quit. Unfortunately, there are times when it is better to leave than to stay.

If you decide that quitting is your only alternative then be prepared to follow the proper procedure: You should resign both *verbally* and in *writing*. So, prepare a resignation letter for the supervisor and for the Human Resources Department. (See a sample resignation letter on page 144.)

Your written resignation should be brief, to the point, and positive. *Never put your negative thoughts on paper.* The written document will be included in your personnel file and could have a longer lasting effect on your career than the individuals or circumstances you are presently dissatisfied with.

A written resignation reinforces the fact that you are leaving and not posing a threat to the company. Also, it gives you the opportunity to communicate what you want to say without being interrupted or sided-tracked by unexpected or unsolicited remarks that can occur during your oral resignation.

Now, for the oral resignation; it should be well thought out and presented with courtesy. Carefully choose your selection of words. You do not want to be misunderstood by — nor responsible for burning bridges with — the people you are leaving. If asked by your current employer or company representative why you are quitting give a positive answer. (At this point whatever you say is going to be viewed as biased.) If the opportunity permits — but only if you feel it is safe to do so — offer suggestions to help the organization operate more effectively. *Do not say or do anything that you may regret later.* Keep in mind that offering constructive criticism can be damaging to your career, therefore, carefully consider your intent and words before speaking. Recall that we spoke of the importance of first impressions in Chapter 5? Well, people also remember *last* impressions, and you want their perception of you to be favorable and positive. After all, you never know when you might *need* a reference from that company or one of its personnel in the future.

It is polite and, above all, *ethical* to give the employer at least a *two week's* notice. Be certain to complete all of your unfinished tasks. Do not discuss your circumstances or discontent with co-workers and peers. Continue to be sensitive to others and keep your conversations positive and constructive. Before departing spend time nurturing your working relationships; you never know whose path you may cross in the future. In other words, always leave with a positive image.

Note:
Sample of a <u>resignation letter</u> is on the following page.

January 17, 2002

B. Ball, Owner
Fine Food Store
5050 West Way
Peaceful, Ohio 56234

Dear Mr. Ball,

I am extremely grateful for the 12 months I have worked
for this Fine Food Store. The time employed here has
been instrumental to my career and professional development. I sincerely hope that my time with you has like-
wise contributed to the progress and growth of Fine
Foods. I am grateful for the opportunity to work with the
caliber of professionals at this store, and for the support
I have received from upper management.

In order that I may continue in the same professional development, I wish to formally announce my resignation. My
last day with Fine Food Store will be February 2, 2002.

So that the transition is a smooth one, I offer my assistance to those individuals who will inherit my duties and
responsibilities.

Sincerely,

David Vernon
123 Friendship Drive
Peaceful, Ohio 45678
(216) 231-2277

*Never be afraid to leave an undesirable situation,
but remember to leave gracefully and ethically;
do not burn the bridges of your future career...*

Conclusion

*This book will help
put your foot in the
next door you try!*

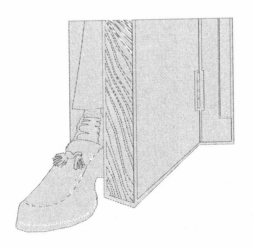

Conclusion

Overview

In conclusion, the author's intentions are for you, the job seeker, to understand that no one is trying to change you. However, in order to conduct a successful job search and land that desired job or get the breaks you need to succeed, you must be willing to make some changes on your own. Society has expectations and unwritten rules that you must be aware of and willing to adhere to in order to be successful.

The purpose of this book is to give you a thorough understanding and introduction to the job search process, to inform you of the actions you need to take to become successful, and equip you with the tools needed for conquering situations encountered as they apply to your particular job search.

After reading this book your confidence should have increased, the rumors and stories should no longer have any value, and you should be ready to go out and conquer that job.

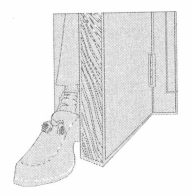

And if you follow the common rules set by the "work society" you are moving into, I know, with all my heart, that you will be successful.

My blessings go with you.

You will go a long way based on the mere
fact that you took the time to read this book.
Now that you have the job search skills,
information, and knowledge you can
see success around the corner...

So, go out there and get it!

Quick Order Form

Telephone orders: Call 1-210-945-8644

E-mail orders: www.newbeeginnings.com

Postal orders: New Bee-ginnings
P.O. Box 545, Universal City, Texas 78148

Please send more *free* information on:

❐ Other books   ❐ Workshops

❐ Speaking Engagements

Name: _____

Address: _____

City: _____ State: _____ Zip: _____

Telephone: _____

E-mail address: _____

Book price: $19.95

Sales tax: Add 8.5% for products shipped.

Shipping charge in U.S.: $4.99 for first book

Payment: ❐ Cheque   ❐ Money Order

Practice Application Form

Personal Information

Last Name	First	Middle	Today's Date
Present Address			Home Phone
City, State, Zip			Social Security Number

Job Information

Position Applied For		Pay Expected
Have you ever worked with us before?		Date available for work.
Hours Available	Will you work overtime?	How were you referred to us?
Are you willing to travel?	Do you have a valid driver's license?	Are you a U.S. Citizen?

Do you have a physical condition which may limit your ability to perform the job you are applying for? If yes, describe.

Person to notify in case of emergency	Phone

Education

Schools Attended	# Yrs. Attended	City & State	Subjects Studied	Avg Grades
Sr. High				
Jr. High				
Grammar				

List any memberships in professional or civic organizations

Employment History

Company name	Phone	Company name	Phone
Address	Month/Year Employed	Address	Month/Year Employed
Name of Supervisor	Wage	Name of Supervisor	Wage
Job Title	Reason for leaving	Job Title	Reason for leaving
Duties		Duties	

May we contact your current supervisor?

References (list below at least three persons, not related to you, whom you have known at least one year)

Name	Address	Position	Phone	Yrs. Known
Name	Address	Position	Phone	Yrs. Known
Name	Address	Position	Phone	Yrs. Known

Printed in the United States
16990LVS00003B/19-27